CASES IN HOLISTIC

Serving with the Poor in Asia

Tetsunao Yamamori, Bryant L. Myers and David Conner, editors

MARC

A division of World Vision International
121 East Huntington Drive, Monrovia, California 91016-3400 USA

SERVING WITH THE POOR IN ASIA

Tetsunao Yamamori, Bryant Myers and David Conner, editors

ISBN 0-912552-90-5

Published by MARC, a division of World Vision International, 121 East Huntington Drive, Monrovia, California 91016-3400, U.S.A.

Printed in the United States of America. Editing and page layout: Ken Graff. Cover design: Richard Sears.

Contents

Part three – Conclusion

Appendixes

Editors and contributors

Tetsunao Yamamori (book co-editor and author of chapter ten) is president of Food for the Hungry International. He served as steering committee chairman for the Chiang Mai consultation. He was born in Nagoya, Japan, where he received his early education. After moving to the United States he obtained a B.D. from Texas Christian University and a Ph.D. from Duke University. He has to his credit eight books and numerous journal articles in missiology, sociology and international development.

Bryant L. Myers (book co-editor and author of chapters twelve and thirteen) is Vice President for Mission and Evangelism in World Vision International and also Director of MARC (Mission Advanced Research and Communication Center). He is a member of the Administrative Committee of the Lausanne Committe for World Evangelization and is co-chair of Lausanne's Theology and Strategy Working Group. He has a Ph.D. from UCLA in biochemistry.

David Conner (book co-editor) is director of Food for the Hungry International, Thailand and served as Chiang Mai consultation coordinator. A graduate of Wheaton College and its graduate school, he is currently a doctoral candidate in adult continuing education at Northern Illinois University. He has facilitated numerous seminars and conferences throughout his career while working with Wheaton College, Food for the Hungry, Billy Graham Center and United Nations High Commissioner for Refugees.

Edgar Metzler (author of chapter one) began his duties as executive director of United Mission to Nepal on February 18, 1990, which happened to be the day the campaign for democracy in Nepal began. He has served on assignments with the Mennonite Central Committee and the Mennonite Board of Missions in various countries in Asia and had earlier served as a Peace Corps director in India, Nepal, Iran and Thailand. He has graduate degrees in theology and international relations and has also served as a pastor.

James Gustafson (chapter two) is a missionary with the Evangelical Covenant Church since 1971 and has served in Thailand in various capacities over the past twenty years. He founded the

Center for Church Planting and Church Growth in 1977, the Issaan Development Foundation in 1983 and the Institute for Sustainable Development in 1991. He earned M.Div and Th.M. degrees from Fuller Theological Seminary and is now working on a Ph.D. in development studies at the University of Wisconsin, Madison.

Jeff Palmer (chapter three) is an agriculturist by training and vocation. He serves as a missionary with the Southern Baptist Convention in the Philippines; his assignment is community development. He lives and works at the Mindanao Baptist Rural Life Center in the village of Kinuskusan, Davao del Sur, Philippines.

Margot Sluka (chapter four) was born and raised in a devout Catholic home in Austria and became a U.S. resident after graduating from Westmont College and UCLA. She taught anthropology at the college level and has research and primary health care experience in Somalia. She has managed World Vision's Oudong Rural Health Project in Cambodia for the past 18 months.

Tri Budiardjo (chapter four) was born in 1952 in Bandung, Indonesia, from a Muslim and Javanese mysticism background. He became a Christian during his high school years, which led to study at the Higher School of Theology in Malang. He has served for more than ten years as a development practitioner with World Vision in diverse cultural settings. For the past two years he has been the organization's field ministries manager in Cambodia.

David Bussau (chapter five) is an Australian businessman who disposed of his business ventures at the age of 35 years and founded the Maranatha Trust. He lived in Asia from 1975 to 1981 and created holistic ministries within the marketplace that applied commercial business principles as expressions of kingdom values. These programs are now activities of the Opportunity Foundation Ltd., of which he is the founder and CEO.

George Stephen (chapter six) is pastor-in-charge of the Presbyterian Church (Scots' Kirk) in Kandy, Sri Lanka. In 1979 he resigned his employment as a senior executive at National Paper Corporation of Sri Lanka and joined the Kandy City Mission, where he served as dean of theological education by extension. He went to Manchester University in U.K. for further theological education.

Scott Geisinger (chapter seven) is an ordained pastor of Calvary Chapel, Santa Barbara, California. He and his wife Anita worked in India with a ministry of the Emmanuel Hospital Association in the Garhwal region of Uttar Pradesh. They then joined Youth With A Mission's Himalaya Social Service in Shimla to train Nepali church leaders and oversee the planting of new house churches among other labor communities.

Paul Hiebert (chapter eight) was born and raised in India, the son of missionary parents. He and his wife served in India as missionaries with the Mennonite Brethren Mission Board. He has served in several prominent academic posts in anthropology and mission and is currently with Trinity Evangelical Divinity School. He is a prolific writer and serves on several mission boards.

Vinay K. Samuel (chapter nine) served as a pastor of the Church of South India in Bangalore and as director of the Evangelical Fellowship of India Committee for Relief. He is executive director of the International Fellowship of Evangelical Mission Theologians, Oxford, U.K. With Chris Sugden, he founded and directs the Oxford Centre for Mission Studies. He co-edits the journal *Transformation: An International Evangelical Dialogue on Mission and Ethics.*

Edgar J. Elliston (chapter eleven) is Associate Professor of Leadership and Development in the School of World Mission, Fuller Theological Seminary. Before going to Fuller in 1986, he worked for 18 years in Africa with Christian Missionary Fellowship; his roles included evangelism, training and development. He holds a Ph.D. in education and cross-cultural communication from Michigan State University.

Introduction

Tetsunao Yamamori

The present volume, *Serving with the Poor in Asia,* is a product of a consultation held in Chiang Mai, Thailand, in November 1994. Forty-nine practitioners, theorists and observers met to discuss cases of effective holistic ministry in Asia and lessons learned. The appendix of this book includes the list of consultation participants and the guidelines for writing the case studies.

Seven cases were selected according to content and geographical representation to appear in this book. Five reflective chapters then examine the cases from perspectives of missionary anthropology, theology, mission strategy, leadership and modernity.

What is holistic ministry?

Many different phrases have been coined to express the concept of holistic ministry, such as:

- Ministry to the whole person
- Holistic and "wholistic" ministry[1]
- Christian social transformation
- Ministering to both physical and spiritual needs
- Integrated development (meaning an integration of evangelism with social action)

Indeed, there is confusion about what holistic ministry is. In a 1988 article in World Vision's journal *Together,* Bryant Myers defined a holistic ministry as "one in which compassion, social transformation, and proclamation are inseparably related."[2] He rightly emphasizes the inseparable nature of evangelism and social action.

The emphasis upon inseparability alone without maintaining the distinction between the two, however, may cause some

1

confusion. For example, in a keynote speech on evangelism at the Nairobi Assembly of the World Council of Churches in 1975, Bishop Mortimer Arias of the Evangelical Methodist Church of Bolivia stressed the holistic approach. He enumerated fourteen kinds of activities in which the World Council of Churches has been engaged since its inception. Without clearly distinguishing which were evangelism and which were social action, Arias then declared: "All this is mission, and it can be an integral part of true evangelism in the world today."[3]

Clearly, both ministry to the soul and ministry to the body are integral to the church's work. But they are different tasks. Evangelism includes those efforts devoted to the proclamation of the Good News of God's salvation in Jesus Christ. These activities bring men and women under the lordship of Christ and result in a vertical relationship with God. Social action encompasses those efforts devoted to the liberation of men and women from social, political and economic shackles. The results of these activities are peace, order and harmony on the horizontal plane. A truly holistic ministry defines evangelism and social action as functionally separate, relationally inseparable and essential to the total ministry of the church.

To be sure, other consultations on holistic ministry have helped increase the visibility of the issue. What has yet to be explored, however, is documenting examples of effective holistic ministry (i.e., development projects that result in the formation of Christ groups) based on empirical data rather than plans, intentions and untested strategies. In this regard, those of us who planned the Chiang Mai consultation felt it imperative for the holistic ministry practitioners to speak to one another. This they did— not only for their own benefit but for the benefit of us all.

God's strategic labor force

Holistic ministry practitioners are God's strategic labor force for today and tomorrow. It is true that the forces of Christianity, and specifically the results of mission outreach in this century, have combined to reduce the number of non-Christians per serious

Christian believers from a ratio of 50 to 1 in 1900 to less than 7 to 1 in 1994. And that ratio continues to drop.

However, despite the opportunities created by the collapse of the Soviet Union and the openness of Eastern Europe, there will still be a massive and growing body of non-Christians in the world utterly outside the reaches of traditional missionary approaches. The fact of today's mission context is that people suffering physically and those yet to know Christ as their Lord are living in geographical areas where traditional missionaries are not allowed but where holistic ministry practitioners are welcomed.

The subject of holistic ministry demands further exploration, especially in using empirical data to examine various models of development work that lead to the formation of Christ groups. As yet, such an examination remains at a pioneering stage. We need more case studies representing various circumstances, various types of development work and various continents. After all this, we will have some accurate information of how effective holistic ministry yields desired goals. The church and missions everywhere await the discovery of such knowledge to help them be faithful in carrying out the Great Commission.

Those who took part in the Asia Consultation on Holistic Ministry are pioneers in search of knowledge that may unlock the secret of an evangelistic approach—knowledge that is desperately needed for today's and tomorrow's mission context. I pray that God will use the materials in this book to increase the effective implementation of holistic ministry in the cause of Jesus Christ.

Acknowledgments

How do you thank people who are your constant ministry companions? Howard and Roberta Ahmanson are just such people to me—and to many others—by allowing us to do projects that are not easily fundable. One day last year, Howard and I were joined by Steve Ferguson, Howard's senior program officer at Fieldstead and Co., for a brainstorming session that resulted in the Asia Consultation on Holistic Ministry. I wish to thank Howard and Roberta for making a generous grant that allowed the consultation to take place and also for their assigning Steve Ferguson and Cristina Houtz to work closely with me along the way.

The consultation steering committee guided the whole process of the Asia consultation and will remain together for other consultations yet to be implemented. With thanks gratitude their ready assistance and encouragement, I wish to recognize the committee members: Don Stephens (Mercy Ships), Fred Gregory (World Concern), Bryant Myers (World Vision International) and Steve Ferguson and Cristina Houtz (Fieldstead and Co.).

With little time in which to plan and execute the Asia consultation, I turned to David Conner, Thailand Director of Food for the Hungry International, to serve as consultation coordinator. He did a superb job, ably assisted by his staff members Kathereeya Robertson and Mr. and Mrs. David Riggins.

The participants—practitioners, theorists and observers—made the consultation the big success it turned out to be. Everyone actively participated in the consultation. Though there were the usual disagreements and differences of opinion, the atmosphere of the consultation was one of affirmation, mutual respect and enthusiastic learning. I am grateful to all who joined us at Chiang Mai.

Finally, I wish to express my gratitude to MARC for publishing this book in such an expeditious way. I am grateful to Jack Kenyon, World Vision International's director of publications. He was easy to work with, and I appreciate his editorial assistance.

NOTES

1   In this book, we are using "holistic" rather than "wholistic" in compliance with our publisher's editorial practices.

2   Bryant L. Myers, "Where are the Poor and the Lost?" *Together* (October-December 1988).

3   Mortimer Arias, "That the World May Believe," *International Review of Mission*. Vol. 65, January 1976, pp. 13-46.

Part one

Case Studies

1
United Mission to Nepal

Edgar Metzler

A veteran missionary with over two decades of service with the United Mission to Nepal (UMN) was asked to make a presentation on holistic ministry. He replied that he wouldn't know what to say, but he was sure UMN had been doing it for the past forty years! As an observer of UMN for thirty years and its executive director since early 1990, I have seen evidence of the truth of his response.

Since 1954, UNM educators, doctors, engineers, agriculturists, foresters, and other technically qualified professionals have accepted the invitation of His Majesty's Government of Nepal to join in the development of one of the world's poorest nations. They have maintained a caring quality in their relationships. They have made significant contributions to nation-building. They have attempted to incarnate the Christ-life in their character and values. They have quietly shared their faith and have been personally involved in the emerging first-generation church. These professionals have fulfilled the purpose of UMN, as stated in its constitution:

> To minister to the needs of the people of Nepal in the Name and Spirit of Christ, and to make Christ known by word and life, thereby strengthening the universal Church in its total ministry.

Background: the country

Nepal, a nation of 20 million, is near the bottom on all development indicators. The annual per capita income has declined slightly in the last few years and now stands at US$160. The maternal mortality rate is a horrendous 850 deaths per 100,000 live births. The overall grain production might be enough to make the country self-sufficient in food, but the rugged terrain and lack of transport results in chronically food-deficient areas.

The past forty years has seen extensive foreign aid attention to Nepal's basic needs. There have been some improvements, such as life expectancy and literacy, although less than 15 percent of females are literate. Some observers question whether the dependency syndrome resulting from that aid may cancel out whatever benefits may have resulted.

Nepal has few natural resources apart from hydropower potential and magnificent scenery. The terrain ranges from the narrow strip of fertile plains along the Indian border, to the middle hills where most of the people live, to the northern range of Himalayan peaks. Nepal has 240 peaks over 20,000 feet. Nepal's geographical position, a rectangle about 500 miles long and 100 miles south to north, sandwiched between India and China, has always defined its main political and diplomatic challenge. Nepal's answer to that challenge was isolation and closed borders. That policy began to change in 1951. The first road into the Kathmandu Valley was completed only in 1956.

The isolation had been deliberate policy of the hereditary prime ministership of the Rana family, who ruled Nepal as a private fiefdom more than a hundred years. The king, considered an incarnation of the Hindu god Vishnu, had no effective control. He was restored to full power in 1951. After a one year experiment with an elected parliament in 1960, the king decided the country wasn't ready for democracy and banned political parties. This was lifted in April 1990 after several months of mostly nonviolent demonstrations that the government's fierce suppression could not finally control.

A new constitution was adopted November 9, 1990. Parliament was elected the following year. The skills and habits of democracy develop slowly, and no government can perform economic miracles in a country at the state of development of Nepal.

The government fell in July 1994, and new elections were held November 15. The communist coalition won the most seats by a narrow margin and by the first week of December had formed a minority government. As the first elected communist government since the end of the cold war, it appears as an anomaly on the world scene. But it is not expected to introduce radical new policies, as its hold on power is so precarious.

Nepal's diverse cultures, many languages, and ethnic groups have coexisted in relative harmony. The Nepalis, generally tolerant and accepting of religious differences, share Hindu temples and Buddhist stupas, each containing images and artifacts of the other religion. The Hindu caste system is officially abolished but still adds to the division of peoples along caste, religious, ethnic and social lines.

Most social scientists are suspicious of census figures that indicate over 80 percent Hindus, less than 15 percent Buddhist, three percent Moslem and two percent others. With the advent of democracy in 1990, a new assertiveness emerged among Buddhists and the various ethnic groups of the hills, which some scholars now claim have only a thin veneer of Hindu culture introduced a few centuries ago. This growing ethnic consciousness is becoming an increasingly significant dimension of the political and religious scene in Nepal.

Background: the church

When Nepal cautiously began to welcome the outside world in 1951, there were a few Christians in the border areas. Ethnic Nepali Christians in Darjeeling, India, on Nepal's eastern border, and many Western missionaries along the southern border had prayed for years for the opening of Nepal to the gospel. Nepali Bible translation had been going on since the first efforts of William Carey.

A few South Indian Christian technicians, working in Indian aid projects, started a congregation in Kathmandu. Soon Nepali-speaking Christians from Darjeeling arrived, and the church was planted.

Church growth was slow due to the hostile cultural and political environment. Nepal was (and still is) the world's only official Hindu kingdom, although the king's divine status seems somewhat diminished since 1990 when he became merely a constitutional monarch.

Until November 1990, changing religion was illegal. The law authorized severe penalties for attempting to convert another person. Christians were jailed for voluntarily changing their religion and for engaging in normal church activities. After the king allowed political parties, the interim government in June 1990 released 30 Christian prisoners serving jail sentences and dismissed more than 150 cases pending against other believers.

The new constitution adopted in November 1990 and the human rights legislation passed in 1991 were a definite improvement for Nepali Christians. But the new law continues the prohibition against anyone attempting to convert another person. The penalties for foreigners include deportation. The cultural bias against conversion remains strong. Just below the surface of the more liberal political atmosphere is a strong Hindu fundamentalist concern about the growth of the church.

Nepali Christians have certainly felt a new sense of freedom since 1990. The church has expanded rapidly, although no accurate figures are available. In 1989, church leaders estimated there were at least 25,000 baptized Christians in the country. Now estimates range from 100,000 to 200,000 believers, with probably half of those baptized.

The Nepali Christians have strong and active evangelistic zeal. The AD2000 conference in Kathmandu October 16-21, 1994, with 1100 present from all sections of the country, gave further impetus to the energetic growth of the church and provided a much-needed model in Christian unity and cooperation. One of the costs of religious freedom has been the loss of the unity the church had known through persecution. The development of quasi-denominational groupings in Nepal and the influence of outside groups wanting to establish a foothold in the country has weakened the cooperative spirit. This has diminished the witness of the unity of the body of Christ and wasted scarce resources in the duplication of services and programs.

The most urgent need is training of pastoral leadership at the basic level, to nurture the many new believers who have only the minimum notion of the meaning and implications of the faith. The involvement of the church in service and nation building are as yet the concern and vision of only a very few.

Background: the United Mission to Nepal

An unexpected invitation from His Majesty's Government to establish a hospital in the chief western town of Tansen and to begin clinics in the Kathmandu Valley was taken up by eight mission agencies working in India, thus was UMN founded in 1954. The number of member bodies has now increased to 39 agencies from 16 countries. The work expanded from health services to education, industrial development and rural development. The staff working in about 35 projects and related organizations totals more than 2,000 Nepalis and about 200 expatriates (plus spouses and families).

Diversity characterizes UMN. The expatriate staff represents many nations, languages and denominational and theological backgrounds. The range of activities includes nonformal education and Freiriean type community development in remote districts, the design and construction of multimillion US dollar (US$) hydropower plants, the operation of four hospitals and a nursing school, and individual secondments into significant positions in government policy formation and educational institutions.

An institutional approach seemed the appropriate response in the beginning when the Mission was asked to address needs for which Nepal had no infrastructure. Now the emphasis is on developing Nepali capacity and implementing the long-standing policy of evolving UMN projects into Nepali hands. A strong commitment from the beginning to train Nepalis in technical and professional leadership has resulted in many competent Nepali staff assuming senior roles in UMN management.

Holistic ministry opportunities, constraints

The Government of Nepal has never given visas for church-related work and is unlikely to do so in the foreseeable future. The general agreement between the ministry of foreign affairs and UMN, renewed every five years, has always contained a clause stipulating that "UMN expatriates shall not engage in any political activities or proselytizing" and that they should not engage in any activities outside those approved in the specific project agreements.

While there is now somewhat more freedom for Nepali Christians, the legal situation has not changed for expatriates. However, the new democratic openness has allowed UMN to be more explicit in its Christian identity. The new government has been positive about UMN because it recognizes the effective implementation of its development programs.

The shape of holistic ministry in Nepal

From the beginning, missionaries assigned to UMN knew that the basis for their visas was their technical and professional expertise and that there were restrictions on overt Christian witness. Yet they came convinced that through their work and relationships the kingdom of God would be expanded and the gospel shared by "word and life." The missionaries lived out their calling in faithfulness to the living Lord, and it made a difference.

What difference? Despite the restrictions, *in every place UMN had a project, a church emerged.* How did this happen? The following are some of the contributing factors:

- Nepali culture was essentially religious; religion could be discussed openly.
- The Bible was available in the Nepali language.

  Nepali (or, in the early days, Indian) Christian staff were included in the project.
- The missionaries learned the language and culture.
- They usually lived in community homes rather than on compounds.

- They opened their homes to Nepali friends, neighbors and co-workers, for language lessons, or to learn hand-icrafts, nonformal education, or simply to share their faith with those who inquired.

- They demonstrated Christian values in personal life and in project activities (e.g., no caste distinctions).

- Without taking formal leadership roles, they responded to needs and opportunities, such as serving on church committees, teaching and preaching when requested, helping to form women's groups, etc.

- They developed close personal relationships with household helpers, neighbors, and other staff.

- They respected Nepali preferences in worship expression, e.g., sitting on the floor, Nepali music (mainly South Asian tunes and indigenous texts).

The situations in the projects varied a great deal. Some fellowships that started with informal Bible studies in missionary homes slowly grew into established congregations. Others struggled for years. Political sensitivities varied from time to time and place to place. Even now there are locations where overly overt Christian activities could jeopardize the support of local authorities.

A significant development in the last several years is that, increasingly, Nepali Christians will already be active in the areas into which UMN projects move. Or the churches will try to send workers into a new project area. Nepali Christian staff can be a resource for Christian witness and presence.

National level

By mutual agreement, the Nepali church and the Mission have maintained separate organizational identities. Many believe the restrictions placed on expatriates over the years have been a blessing in promoting the development of an indigenous church. UMN is known by the Nepali public as a Christian organization and its contribution to nation building has been recognized. This has helped establish a credibility for Christians. At least five times in the past four years I have heard high government officials, including the prime minister, state that what Nepali government staff and development workers need is more of "the missionary spirit."

Several months ago I was talking with the Israeli ambassador at the reception for Israel's national day. One of the highest government officials thanked the ambassador for the practical and effective aid projects Israel had sponsored over the years. He said, "The work of your people here has established a good reputation for your nation," and then turning toward me he continued, "just as the work of UMN has made a good reputation for Christianity."

Umbu Village

Okhaldhunga is a remote district in Eastern Nepal, three days' walk from the nearest road and four hours from an airstrip. A 30-bed hospital was established there 30 years ago and a community health and development program soon after. Later the development section evolved into an extensive, integrated rural development program.

Satoshi Mori, a Japanese agriculturist who had worked in the project several years, proposed that he and his family relocate to Umbu village, about a day's walk from Okhaldhunga. They would operate there basically on their own, with monthly visits to Okhaldhunga for project staff meetings.

The family lived in Umbu for seven years. By the time they left, the village had made significant progress in development areas such as drinking water, crop and animal productivity, nutrition, literacy, and education. A church was established with local leadership. The church building was identified by a cross on the outside, probably for the first time in Nepal.

Why and how did it happen? Some of the contributing factors include:

- Satoshi and Masako had a clear vision of their roles as missionaries incorporating both development activities and sharing of their faith.
- They had a long-term commitment to remain in a remote village until confidence and trust were

developed, resulting in both sustainable development and indigenous church leadership.

- They had excellent language fluency, including learning the local dialect.
- Masako made a special contribution to development through children's education.
- They took an approach to development that maximized community cooperation and participation in utilizing local resources and local control.
- They accepted a village level lifestyle, living very much with the people.
- The village really liked the Satoshi family.
- They were far enough away from the district center that government officials didn't really know or care what was happening.

The seven years certainly had problems and challenges, such as having little control over their time (especially with family), balancing the demands of development activities and the growing church fellowship, and the maintenance of health. The Moris left two years ago, and the transformation in Umbu appears to be continuing. There will be further evaluation done to learn from this experience.

Jhimruk

The UMN strategy for industrial development in Nepal began with the establishment of the first technical school in the country in 1963. Later, private limited companies were established. The goal was to help the companies become self-reliant in terms of management, technical competence and financial stability. UMN would then withdraw as the companies matured to stand on their own.

The largest of the nine companies established were three involved in various aspects of hydropower development. They were engaged to undertake the construction of a 12-megawatt hydropower plant to be built with a US$22 million grant from the Norwegian government.

15

The first UMN missionaries arrived at the remote site in June 1990. By January 1991 the adult expatriate team had grown to 17. During 1991, several Nepali Christians moved to the site, only five of them baptized believers.

During the early months of the project there were several strikes. Strike leaders made public accusations against the missionaries, warning of the "cow-eating foreign religion." This period of difficulty strengthened the resolve of the team to engage in prayer. Because of the public attitudes, there was caution in early Christian activities. The few Nepalis met weekly in the home of a Nepali Christian engineer and the expatriates met on another night in one of their homes.

The first public Christian activity was to celebrate Christmas in 1990 with Christmas carols in the project and in the nearby bazaar. From January 1991 a regular weekly worship service for both Nepalis and expatriates was started in the home of the Nepali engineer. A church committee was formed. The "Jesus" film was shown to company staff and local people. An outdoor sunrise service was conducted. A women's fellowship began and helped nurture new believers.

A major concern from the beginning was the need to develop mature local leadership before the project's four-year completion date. Several visits were arranged for ministry by Nepali church leaders. By November 1991 three house fellowships were meeting weekly. Christmas that year saw an expanded program of reaching out to local communities.

In February 1992 there were the first baptisms ever in that district. Ten believers joined the church. Only two were local residents; the others were company staff working at the project.

During 1992 there were further visits by Christian resource persons and attendance at training conferences elsewhere by the Jhimruk Christians. This was all aimed at helping the local church become mature enough to continue when the expatriates would begin leaving in 1993.

In March of 1993 another group of eight was baptized. The church was meeting in rented quarters. During 1993 the expatriate team began to be transferred, along with some of the mature Christian staff. The last expatriate left in March 1994. Soon after, the rented room was given up and the few remaining local families met in homes. Finally only one local family was left.

At the end of four years, there was no permanent local church. However, through the presence of the project many had become Christians, quite a few were baptized, but almost all moved on to other areas for reasons of employment. Many are praying that the seeds planted at Jhimruk will still grow into a strong indigenous church.

How to evaluate this experience?

- Was four years in that situation long enough to plant and nurture a church fellowship?

- Could national church groups have taken more responsibility for continuing the work? Although there are trained Christian workers in the capital city, none were willing to move to this remote area.

- How did the Christian staff, expatriate and Nepali, view their presence at Jhimruk? Was the hydropower project simply the cover for them to be there to make a Christian witness? Was there a way to conceptualize and articulate a vision of hydropower development as part of God's mission, of God's redeeming power transforming human society? Certainly the Christian staff believed that in some way God had been at work through the witness of their word and life.

- The design of this project focused only on the power plant with little attention to the impact on the total welfare of the community. Would a more integrated community development approach have presented a more attractive project face to the local people? That would have involved a commitment to stay in the area for a longer time.

17

- Many of the Nepali and expatriate Christian engineering staff moved on to a new hydropower project in another remote area. This project would seem to be off to a better start, as there was consultation with the local community and the Nepali church before the project began. Christian workers are now in the area and are giving leadership to the church planting efforts, as happened in Jhimruk. Here again the vision of industrial development as part of God's work in Nepal needs to be addressed. Otherwise it becomes only a means of getting some expatriate Christians into a remote, unreached location—an honorable goal, but is it enough?

- At the new site there has been a concerted effort to involve the community in mitigating the impact of the project and assuring that the local community benefits.

A Nepali church NGO

Under the new government, there has been an explosion of local non-government organizations. It is relatively easy for NGOs to receive official recognition. It remains to be seen how much impact the hundreds of new NGOs will have, but it is too soon to judge. UMN has a project to support a select group of local NGOs.

One possibility raised by the legislation on NGOs was that UMN could register a Christian NGO and gain the legal means for direct cooperation with the church. This has now been done, although the registration papers describe development goals without specific reference to the church. This NGO is sponsored by the National Church Fellowship of Nepal, the largest coalition of churches in the country. UMN seconded a senior Nepali Christian development worker for three years to help the NGO get started and also arranged some funding from UMN member bodies directly to the NGO.

The project area is a remote, rugged area that has had very little development activity. Main activities to date have been nonformal education and a suspension walking bridge to enable some remote villages to have access to the outside world during the monsoon season.

The church is growing rapidly among the dominant ethnic group of the area. In some villages a majority of the residents are calling themselves Christians. Much of this interest is credited to the healing ministry that is widespread in that area. At this point, the Christian NGO sees its main purpose to be improving the life of the new Christian communities.

Some questions

- While encouraging the local church to develop a holistic vision of ministry, is it realistic to assist them in a model derived mainly from a long-standing foreign organization with external resources of finance and personnel?

- Development projects require competent management. This skill is in short supply in Nepal. Should UMN strategy give more attention to management training as the first step in assisting in development ministries with the local church?

- Cross-cultural skills are also necessary for national Christians moving to new areas of work within their own country. Highly trained urban Christians often do not want to live and work in remote areas. They may dominate local people in work and church matters in a "colonial" manner. What kind of training will shape the right attitudes and leadership styles?

- "Small is beautiful" is probably a good motto for an emerging first-generation church embarking on social ministries. How can UMN, from the perspective of its "bigness" give more priority to working with the church to design appropriate-scale projects to fit the administrative capacity of its church partners?

UMN's future holistic ministry

If the founders of UMN had come to Nepal without restrictions on their activities, they would undoubtedly, sooner or later, have established hospitals and schools, just as they did in India. But their strategy was determined by the government. Nevertheless, faith was shared and the gospel made manifest by word and work and life. We thank God that even though the missionaries may not have articulated a thorough missiology of holistic ministry, God used their faithful efforts to make known the divine love and establish and build the church of Jesus Christ.

In the last two years we have developed a statement of values, making explicit and visible convictions that were always there. The process of developing the values with the participation of a multi-faith staff was a constructive process of team building. I believe the values help make specific God's goal for the kingdom, for the re-creation of all creation. We are trying to find ways to make this values statement a living, vital part of organizational life, a common commitment for all staff of different faiths.

The UMN policy from the beginning was that the work would be turned over to Nepali organizations or the government. The assumption had been that the church would not have the resources to take over work that UMN had started. There were simply so few Nepali Christians with the technical and managerial skills needed. We hope and pray that their numbers will increase. We are now finding ways to assist Nepali Christians in the training they need for such leadership, but we find ourselves in a challenging dilemma.

Through vigorous implementation of one of the three original purposes of UMN—"to train the people of Nepal in professional skills and leadership"—we have developed a large cadre of experienced, well-trained, dedicated workers. But few of them are Christian. What is the role of such staff, especially in leadership positions, in holistic ministry? Do we believe God can also work through such individuals? The question of how an organization such as UMN at this stage of its development and in this environment expresses and maintains its Christian identity is a matter of current discussion and discernment. A policy statement on the Christian identity of UMN was adopted by the board of directors on November 20, 1994.

One area of holistic ministry that has assumed new importance in Nepal is human rights. During the years of the church's persecution, UMN strategy to help our Nepali sisters and brothers was to inform the UMN member bodies in various countries about human rights abuses and ask them to petition their governments to communicate to the Government of Nepal. From personal experience while working in a Washington office, I know that actually happened.

But our Nepali colleagues didn't always understand this strategy. After the revolution, I was asked several times in church meetings how UMN would respond if Christians were again persecuted. I replied that I believe human rights, including religious freedom, are as important to true development as clean water, health care, and good nutrition. Therefore I would take to the highest level of His Majesty's Government any harassment or persecution of the church. I was then asked if I would do that even if it jeopardized the continued presence of UMN in Nepal. My personal reply, not cleared with the board of directors, was that I believe it is that important.

Concern and struggle for human rights must, of course, not be limited to the rights of Christians. An authentic Christian witness would extend to all victims of oppression and discrimination, which in Nepal includes child laborers, lower castes, and women.

The shape and structure for holistic ministry for UMN will change in the future as we work toward the vision which is emerging among us. One way we describe this is:

> Our vision is that Nepali individuals, communities and institutions will serve people of Nepal and carry forward the process of transformation that God intends. Our goal is capacity development, achieved through a strategy of building partnerships with Nepali individuals, communities, and organizations, including the church, to increase their ability and motivation to serve the people of Nepal.

21

The key concepts are *transformation, capacity development* and *partnerships*. In pursing such a vision we need to keep clearly before us the biblical concern for the poor and marginalized in the society, that they too develop the capacity they need. Otherwise it is tempting to work with those already able to improve their future.

In the future vision, UMN as an organization will decrease, Nepali participation in God's dream for Nepal will increase. As that happens, the ministry will be less the United Mission to Nepal, and more the United Mission *in* Nepal.

May God guide us, correct us and strengthen us.

2

Doing the gospel in Northeast Thailand

James Gustafson

In April 1977 the Center for Church Planting and Church Growth (CCPCG) was begun in Udon, Thailand, by one missionary family working for the Evangelical Covenant Church and two Thai families. All three families had worked together with the Church of Christ in Thailand for six years prior to starting CCPCG. The center was formally admitted as a member of the Evangelical Fellowship of Thailand (EFT) the same year.

The ministry was focused on holistic ministry from its inception. The new organization struggled with doing the gospel in Northeast Thailand in a culturally relevant way. By the end of 1977, five churches had been planted in five villages in the province of Udon. During that same period, CCPCG—determined to focus on the agricultural needs of the Northeast Thai rural poor—started on the Udon Patina Farm (a 30-acre integrated agriculture farm on the outskirts of Udon to the north).

In 1983 the Issaan Development Foundation (IDF) was formed as an official Thai nonprofit development foundation. Its purpose has been to focus on the social, economic, physical, techno-logical and organizational needs of the rural Thai poor and, through a "process-broker" approach, to help the poor to experi-ence true development by becoming what God desires them to be in Northeast Thailand. From the beginning, IDF and the CCPCG were organizationally distinct but functionally the same move-ment. IDF currently has departments dealing with a wide variety of issues in rural development (health, sustainable agriculture, mechanics and sewing) as well as urban development (slums in the provincial capitals of Northeast Thailand).

In early 1990 the Institute for Sustainable Development (ISD) was started by CCPCG and the IDF to take the responsibility for doing the research and curriculum development as well as the basic training for the ongoing work of both organizations. It currently focuses on a variety of issues that deal with the work of the CCPCG and the IDF (ethnomusicology, Northeast Thai culture, contextualized theology, communications and Northeast Thai arts, sustainable and integrated agriculture, and sustainable development).

By early 1993 the church had grown to more than 200 local churches and over 3,000 members. It was decided by consensus that CCPCG would be dissolved and the church would take responsibility for running its own internal organization. As a result, CCPCG ceased to exist and the Thailand Covenant Church (TCC) came into existence in its place and is currently a member of the EFT. Both the IDF and the ISD continue to relate to the TCC and to provide a process-broker enablement to the TCC.

Since the start of ISD in 1990, both IDF and ISD have worked to spawn several other organizations that are working in other areas of Thailand in holistic ministry. Before 1990, the Lower Issaan Center for Enablement (LIFE) was begun with two missionary families and ten Thai staff members in Roi-Et, 200 kilometers southeast of Udon. LIFE is now an official foundation registered with the Thai government. Its focus is holistic ministry in the lower Issaan area.

About the same time, a new ministry was started in the slums of Bangkok by staff from IDF. In 1993, a missionary family joined the two Thai families who had begun that work and started the Abundant Life Center (ALC) in Bangkok. ALC is doing holistic ministry similar to the other organizations, but in the area of the urban center of Thailand.

The process of coming to know Christ

From the start of the ministry in 1977, the focus of the ministry was on the process of enabling Jesus Christ to be "born" into Northeast Thai culture. This necessitated a radical departure from just about all that it means to be a Christian in the Western form of Christianity that is prevalent in Thailand. Much time was spent struggling with integrating culture and theology to speak clearly to the Northeast Thai mind.

The team focused on doing the gospel at the grassroots level. Those who were gifted in "holy gab" spent time in the villages talking about Jesus Christ the *Living Word* (similar to the Buddhist concept of *tumma* or word of the Buddha). A concerted effort was made to avoid any relationship to Christianity as understood by the Thai (to be a Christian in Thailand means to give up your Thainess and become Western.) Emphasis was placed on families coming together to accept Christ. Many of the early believers were those who had a strong connection with Buddhism previous to believing in Jesus Christ.

As team members who were gifted in communicating the gospel at the village level were doing one-on-one ministry in the villages, other members of the team were working at developing the culture-theology—contextualized theology and study materials that were used in the ongoing process of grounding the new believers in the Word.

When the ministry reached its second year of operation, the process of communicating the gospel was taken over by the new believers. At that point, all of the team began to focus on the ongoing training of the new believers. This became the basic role of the parachurch organizations as the new believers expanded the church with their own witness to family members and friends. The church began to grow spontaneously and has continued to do so until this time.

A Christ group emerges

So-called development work has not been seen as the way to bring people to Jesus Christ. The development aspect of the ministry of IDF and related organizations has never been the spearhead into a community with the intention to bring people to Christ. Rather, the development aspects of the ministry have always been focused on the church and its immediate community. The concern is to enable the formation of a strong and stable local church which can do the gospel with its own community in a way that is not only culturally relevant and theologically sound, but is also empowered to meet the felt needs of the community in every way.

For IDF, it is important to enable development to serve and not lead in the process of ministering to people in need. The work of development cannot be separated from the work of doing the gospel or of grounding the church in the Word of God. But, for IDF, the introduction of development usually takes place following the community's initial response to the gospel. It will often encompass more than just the church community. (Many of the projects have half believers and half nonbelievers.)

The main factors that have contributed to the response of people to the gospel and the emergence of a local church in the ministry of IDF can be listed briefly:

- *Know the people to be approached.* To know and under-stand the people who are to be approached with the gospel is critical to the communication of that gospel. It demands that the communicator be one of the com-munity he is seeking to reach (in heart and mind if not in fact).

- *Know the gospel.* It is also critical to understand the gospel, what it says, and how it applies to the context of the culture and community to be reached. The gospel is a word about the grace of God. Salvation is in Jesus Christ alone and through faith in the grace of God alone. There is real power in the gospel if it is not watered down with Christian religion and caused to lose its critical content. If people can hear and truly understand the grace of God in Jesus Christ, they can then decide for or against accepting it. When Christian religion is the content of evangelistic efforts, the transforming power of Christ is lacking and the result (even if people believe) is a weak and unstable church.

- *Contextualize the gospel in the local culture.*   Since communication is what is heard in the mind and heart of the listener and not necessarily what is said by the communicator, it is crucial that we do everything we can to make our intended message clear to the listener. The gospel of Jesus Christ must have local cultural forms and expressions to be clearly understood by the local community. IDF and its related organizations have been committed to this process from the start; the results show the effectiveness of the process.

- *Counter the aspects of the local value system that are counter to the values of the gospel.*   In all societies there are values that are counter to the gospel. These must be countered in the love of Christ if the new believers and the church they will form are to be strong and healthy in Christ. IDF has developed an approach of dialogue teaching that involves everyone in the community in the process of learning. It is in such a context that confrontation is best handled. Growth in maturity takes place only as there is a healthy and loving countering of values in the society that are counter to those in the Word of God.

- *Integrate the above elements in the development process.* Development begins in the mind and the heart. If development is to be sustainable it must be part of the mindset and the values of the community. IDF integrates the above points in all aspects of the process of development. This binds new believers into the new community of the church.

Evaluation of the case

A number of things have been obstacles to the progress of the ministry of IDF. These can be listed briefly:

- *The tendency to grow too much.* IDF and ISD grew in their development and consequently in the number of staff to the point at which the concentration of their critical conceptual framework or basic philosophy became watered down. This was especially true in the lives of staff at the periphery of the organizations. Recently the decision was made to modify the size of the organizations. The result has been reconsecration of the basic core beliefs or values of the organizations. We have found that it is important not to grow too big to keep the beliefs of the organization in the hearts and minds of all members of the organization.

- *The temptation to overemphasize financial support.* IDF and ISD, as they have grown in size, have tended to make financial support of the organizations the highest priority. This becomes more and more of a burden until a major part of the organization is focused on financial support rather than on the mission. The IDF is learning to keep the organization at a manageable size and not to let opportunities for increased funding lead to increased larger size organization and operational costs.

- *The failure to relate honestly and counter wrong values in self and others.* There is nothing harder than being honest with one another and countering values that need to be countered. Thai culture has a natural tendency to avoid such encounters, and Western culture is similar. As IDF team members are willing to talk to each other and counter each other in love, to that extent we grow in power for service. As we fail to talk to each other and counter each other in the love of Christ, to that extent we grow weak and useless.

In short, we are people in process who are learning to free God up to be God. We are also learning to depend on him in every area of our lives. There are many other problems with our work that could be mentioned, but they would all come back to the central point: the more we have learned to deny ourselves and to accept our weaknesses and depend on God in every detail, the more we have found his wisdom and strength to be sufficient for all of our needs. This is a tough one, though, and probably the critical cutting edge for all of us on the IDF/ISD team.

NOTES

1   "Integrated Holistic Development and the World Mission of the Church." 1985.

2   "The Integration of Evangelism and Development." 1990.

3   "The Issaan Development Foundation: A Rural Development Approach in Northeast Thailand." 1988.

3

Growing believers in Mindanao, Philippines

Jeff Palmer

T he Philippines Baptist Mission began a new chapter in holistic ministries in 1971 with the start of the Mindanao Baptist Rural Life Center (MBRLC). Agriculture missionary Harold R. Watson had been assigned to teach vocational agriculture at Southern Baptist College, M'Lang, North Cotabato. He left that work to pursue a dream of working more directly with farmers and those whose lives needed a direct touch physically as well as spiritually.

History and background

Rev. Watson and the original staff, including the current farm manager Rodrigo "Rod" Calixtro, began a small ten-hectare demonstration farm intended for use as an extension base for helping local farmers. According to Rev. Watson, with the setting of the first pole for the first building, people began to pass by and ask, "What are you demonstrating here?" Little did the staff know that with these innocent beginnings, within 20 years 20,000 people a year would pass through and ask virtually the same question.

One of the first projects started in the opening year was a small seed production plot and a model of a Food Always in the Home (FAITH) garden. Early farmers' clubs, which were later to be called Christian Farmers' Clubs (CFCs) were established and used as a means to teach simple agricultural skills to local farmers.

In 1972 MBRLC purchased its first dairy goats and began a program that has been highly successful up to the present. A rabbit project and other small animal projects were soon started and the Center began to have more visitors. What started as a small extension farm was becoming a showcase for rural development.

In 1977 Dr. Whirled A. Laquihon, dean of Southern Christian College, joined the Center's staff, and a new era of education and outward focus began. The administration adopted PEDAL (Plan for Expansion, Development and Leadership) that included REDEEM (Research, Education, Development, Extension, Evangelism and Mission), which described and laid the course for MBRLC over the next years. PEDAL also proposed an out-of-school training program for youth, the "Baptist Farmer" periodical, a farm radio program and development of simple farmer-oriented reading materials to disseminate information and technologies developed at the Center. In 1978 MBRLC launched its aggressive agricultural extension program, Christian Farmer's Club and Rural Life Institute. The Center also expanded to its current size of 19 hectares. Also in 1978, the internationally known SALT (Sloping Agricultural Land Technology) project officially began.

In 1979 the Baptist Outside of School Training (BOOST) program, located adjacent to the MBRLC, completed its first training session. Also, the first issue of "The Baptist Farmer" was published; this is still MBRLC's quarterly publication. In October 1980, MBRLC's "Balik Kita sa Uma" ("Back to the Farm") program was first heard on local radio stations in southern Mindanao.

Due to success in ministry to human and spiritual needs, MBRLC was supported by the Philippines Baptist Mission (PBM) to expand to other parts of Mindanao. In 1981, the first satellite program began. Eventually smaller but similar programs took shape in Surigao del Sur, Zamboanga del Sur, Davao City, Agusan del Sur, South Cotabato and lower Davao del Sur.

By the mid-1980s SALT was becoming internationally known. Because of this, Rev. Watson and Dr. Laquihon were featured speakers at a number of developmental seminars. Also, many international visitors began visiting MBRLC; this prompted founding an international branch known as the Asian Rural Life Development Foundation (ARLDF). ARLDF now functions in most Southern Asia and Pacific countries, with training centers or cooperators in the countries of Indonesia, Thailand, India and Bangladesh. Active work and linkages with other groups extend to Sri Lanka, Malaysia, Nepal, Vietnam and Burma. Almost 80 countries worldwide have visited the MBRLC-ARLDF facilities.

Many other technologies were developed along the way. All these were developed along the same lines as the SALT technology:

- Simple
- Easy to adopt
- Easy to duplicate as to inputs and degree of difficulty
- Geared for the local farmer

Some of the technologies include SALT 2 (Simple Agro-Livestock Technology), SALT 3 (Sustainable Agroforest Land Technology), SALT 4 (Small Agrofruit Livelihood Technology) and UPLIFT (Using Properly Lowland Integrated Farming Technology).

Today, MBRLC-ARLDF welcomes more than 20,000 visitors a year. Many of these are one-day visitors coming to see the various farming technologies, purchase seeds/seedlings, ask for information or just to buy fresh goats' milk. About 2,000 people per year are trained for at least one week in the various technologies; about 75 percent of these are farmers. The Center also entertains more than 300 international visitors per year; about half of these are involved in some sort of training.

The staff has grown from two to more than 100. A number of these are field workers. Out of the 100, only three are non-Filipino (from the U.S.A.). All are devoted to the holistic ministry ideals of the Center. About half the staff are professionals. Many of them are young men and women who choose to live in villages as extension agents and propagate the Good News of abundant life physically as well as spiritually. There are four functioning satellite programs with staff dedicated to relieving physical and spiritual suffering.

The Center focuses on three main aspects: agriculture, health care, and Bible training. The agricultural work primarily emphasizes sustainable food production and income generation for the Filipino farm family. The Center's health care program, Farm Family Health, concentrates on nutrition, preventive medicine, sanitation and water development. Bible training using the technique of Chronological Bible Story Telling is interwoven into each program of the Center.

The theme of the Center

From the beginning, the work of the Center has been rooted in John 10:10. Jesus says, "I come that they might have life and have it more abundantly." It has always been the intent of MBRLC to minister to the whole person, physically and spiritually. As ministers of the gospel, we are commanded to touch people where they hurt. If they are blind, we touch their eyes. If they are lame, we touch their legs. If they are hungry, we touch their stomachs. And if they are lost in sin, we touch their hearts with the hope of the Good News of Jesus Christ.

In this sense, all we have done and continue to do at MBRLC is to give a "cup of cold water" in the name of Jesus (Matthew 10:42). We have taken the mandate in Matthew 25:31-46 (the sheep and the goats) as seriously as the mandate in Matthew 28:18-20 (the Great Commission). We do not believe in separating the spiritual from the physical.

The effect of MBRLC on physical suffering relief is well documented. From international awards won by the Center to staff who take pride in their effective community development programs, MBRLC has a proven track record that is recognized by religious and nonreligious organizations, government and nongovernment agencies, and universities and nonformal education entities.

The effect of MBRLC on the alleviation of spiritual suffering is also well documented. More than 50 local churches have been started due to direct ministries of MBRLC. When the "cup of cold water" is given, it is always followed by an explanation that the love of God is the reason for giving. As a ministry of the Philippine Baptist Mission, MBRLC's priorities are determined by the mission purpose statement: "Evangelism that results in churches."

Most of the staff members are actively involved in some local church ministry on their own time. Many are directly involved in church planting; one has been instrumental in starting more than 20 churches. All of the one-week trainees at MBRLC have at least one opportunity to hear and respond to the gospel. Also, the satellite projects are solely devoted to training and developing church leaders in a nine-month training program called TEACH (Tribal Evangelism, Agriculture, Church planting and Health care).

To date, more than 1,000 young people who are church leaders have been trained in the BOOST program. More than 300 pastors and wives have been trained in the comprehensive TEACH program. Now many of these are serving as Baptist Convention leaders and teachers. They also are equipped to be better farmers and pastors where they live and minister.

Factors in evangelism, church planting and growth

The major factor for the emergence of churches and new believers through the development ministry is that from the beginning, this was the purposed outcome. Never has MBRLC consciously used the "carrot on a stick" approach to conversion. Rather, we have used development work to show genuine Christian concern, make contacts and allow the Holy Spirit to work through us in people's lives.

People came to know Christ through our developmental work because we actively incorporated evangelism into our program. The fifth letter of the REDEEM acronym stands for evangelism. We believe that all people are lost and in need of a Savior, namely Jesus Christ. He is the only way to salvation. We have a moral and spiritual obligation to share our beliefs in him. We never do this in a forceful way but only as an invitation for those who wish to know more.

We learned early on that helping a person physically is not necessarily enough. What if a person receives a better income from learning new technology, only to spend more on drinking and gambling? We strongly believe that a person must also develop spiritually.

A second factor for successful spiritual ministries of the MBRLC is the staff. Most staff are mature, highly motivated young Christian men and women. We have tried to cultivate a feeling that each person working with MBRLC is involved in a ministry and not just a job. Therefore, direct community development is seen as a Christian ministry as well as producing seeds and processing milk on the farm.

When hiring new personnel, we always concentrate more on the quality of the person than the qualifications. Our people are highly qualified for their jobs, but they also have a quality to their lives that openly and eagerly testifies to the lordship of Jesus Christ.

The staff is encouraged to feel part of a team in our approach to rural development and evangelization. Organizationally, the professional is not above the field worker, the foreigner missionary is not above the national co-worker, and the extensionist is not better than the trainer who stays mostly at the Center. All are encouraged to see where they fit into the overall vision and organization of MBRLC. All are encouraged to see their work, whether in the field or in training, as a ministry to people.

A third factor for the success of MBRLC in its spiritual ministries is the commitment to initiate community development work through local churches, especially in the entry phase of programs. MBRLC tries to be open and work effectively with other religious groups and other branches of the Christian faith. However, in its extension program, the most common point of entry into a village is a local Baptist church or other body of believers. This has kept the programs of the Center focused and generally allows for some immediate successes in the initial stages of village work because trust has already been established.

Lessons learned

MBRLC has been a good example of holistic Christian ministries seeking to alleviate human suffering in both the physical and spiritual context. However, we have learned some lessons that could make us more effective in spiritual ministry.

The first lesson is that a better climate for community and spiritual development can be obtained if a better overall trust level is established during the initiation of extension projects. As we choose to work through local Baptist churches during initial entry phases, this sometimes hinders our overall impact on the communities as a whole. We are immediately seen as Baptists with Baptist programs and sometimes people are afraid to join in if they are not Baptist themselves. We try to overcome this through trust building, the physical presence of our extensionist and being more community focused in the initiation of projects.

A second lesson learned is that it may be too much to expect the agriculture and health care extensionist to follow up on all of the needs of the community, including deep spiritual needs. In the past, we have resisted hiring pastor-extensionists with the main priority of following up on spiritual needs. We now incorporate a resource person in most of our areas to help in spiritual matters. This pastor-extensionist is available for forming and initially leading house church Bible studies. This person is also available for teaching simple Bible education courses to strengthen local church leaders.

A third lesson learned is the need to network more effectively. In the first years of MBRLC, we were so busy doing what we were good at that there was little time to team up with others. As we continue to grow and expand, we find ourselves more and more in contact with other groups' projects. We feel that this is a course for the future that will serve to increase the spiritual impact of MBRLC. We will give priority to organizations that seek to carry out the Great Commission.

Conclusions

Growth is the key idea in reviewing the history, lessons learned and other aspects of nearly 23 years of holistic Christian ministry by MBRLC. When the organization started out, there was no design or idea that it would ever grow to be what it is today. However, due to the flexibility of the staff and leadership, milestones have been reached along the way but we did not want to rest upon our laurels. Rather, we have continually pressed on and grown. This is a key process for the success of the program: knowing who you are, setting definite goals, laying out plans for the future and then working those plans with flexibility.

The start of the program in 1971 was a milestone for Southern Baptist developmental work around the world. The addition of Dr. Warlito A. Laquihon and his vision for outreach was another turning point.

The latest milestone is the MBRLC vision statement (Appendix 1). These ideas will shape the holistic ministry of MBRLC into and beyond the year 2000.

I appreciate the opportunity to present this case. I hope that the reader will be encouraged and challenged by it. May God bless you as you also seek to join in his work of developing people.

Appendix 1
Vision Statement
Mindanao Baptist Rural Life Center

MINDANAO BAPTIST RURAL LIFE CENTER (MBRLC) is one of the main programs of the Philippine Rural Life Ministry, the agriculture and community development work of the Philippine Baptist Mission (PBM) of the Foreign Mission Board, Southern Baptist Convention, U.S.A. The overall purpose of the Rural Life Ministry is to use agriculture and health care to reach Filipino rural people for Christ, effect church growth and development in rural areas, relieve human suffering caused by agriculture-related problems, improve the health of the rural poor, and train and educate people in stewardship of God's creation.

MBRLC is a nonprofit, church-related, private volunteer organization with public concern. It is a rural human development ministry of the Philippine Baptist Mission, It was opened in September 1971 by missionary-agriculturist Harold R. Watson in Barangay Kinuskusan, Bansalan, Davao de Sur on the island of Mindanao. The original land area of ten hectares has now expanded to 19 hectares.

Scope

The scope of the agricultural ministry includes all hilly and upland farmers in Mindanao-Visayas and throughout the Philippines, with special emphasis on tribal groups.

Vision

In a community where MBRLC has implemented its programs of development, it is envisioned that:

- The community will be organized and capable of discerning its needs and problems and finding solutions that are just and fair for the whole community.
- The people will be educated, self-disciplined, spiritually mature and responsible citizens.
- The community will be fully aware of responsibility to the environment and will practice environmental stewardship.
- The people of the community will experience reasonably good health and be able to help meet the primary health needs of their family and the community.

- There will be a mature, self-propagating Southern Baptist church in the community with a well-equipped pastor and church leaders.
- The farms will be productive and ecologically balanced, conserving land and natural resources in a sustainable way.
- The community will have sufficient supply of food, fuel and potable drinking water.
- The community will have or have access to an Abundant Life Co-op.
- The community will be enthusiastic in propagating the abundant life shared with them.

Mission

MBRLC takes the mandate of living and sharing the Good News of abundant life through a holistic Christian lifestyle.

Purpose

The MBRLC ministry is to help all people, especially hilly and upland farmers, experience abundant life as found in John 10:10b.

General Objective

The MBRLC's general objective is to help redeem people from physical and spiritual poverty.

Specific Objectives

Below are the specific objectives of the MBRLC:

- To research and develop appropriate farming technologies, systems, plants and animals that will help Filipino farmers increase and sustain their production and income.
- To extend these farming practices that have proven to be sustainable to upland farmers, especially tribal groups, on Mindanao and throughout the Philippines.
- To develop appropriate sustainable technologies that farmers see as needed to have sustainable farming systems in the uplands.

- To educate and train farmers and farm families in sustainable farming systems, farm family health, and Christian living.

- To evangelize—enable people understand that God loves them and that he has a purpose and plan for their lives.

- To promote mission—help all farmers, and especially hilly and upland farmers, to have an abundant life.

General strategies

REDEEM expresses the strategies of MBRLC in accomplishing its objectives. It stands for: Research, Education, Development, Extension, Evangelism, Mission

Specific strategies

MBRLC's specific strategies are as follows:

- Maintain *a rural life center.* Purposes include developing and testing technologies for the upland farmer; training farmers, technicians and other interested people in sustainable agriculture; producing good animals, seed, and plants for hilly land and upland farmers; producing literature and radio programs; providing models of sustainable agriculture systems for farmers, technicians, and the general public (including school children and college students) and serving as a base of an extension program.

- Maintain *satellite training centers* in strategically selected areas. The centers train out-of-school youth and church leaders in farming technologies, farm family health, Bible and church growth techniques. The centers also provide models of abundant life for the communities in which these projects are found.

- Maintain *an extension program* in mainly poor tribal locations (impact areas). Implement development efforts in farming, health care, water development, community organizing, cooperatives and church planting.

- Maintain *a farm family health and water development program* that links with the impact areas.

- Maintain *a community development program* that links with churches and extension.
- Maintain *a Baptist Cooperative program* (to be phased out in about five years).

Programs and projects

Specific programs and projects were developed as the need arose. MBRLC became well known because of the following programs and projects:

Programs

Baptist Outside School Training (BOOST) Program

Extension

Training

Back to the Farm radio program and "Baptist Farmer" newsletter

Cooperative Organization and Responsible Enterprises (CORE) program

Farm Family Health

Tribal Evangelism, Agriculture, Church planting and Health care (TEACH) program

Development communication materials production

Pastors in Rural Evangelism, Agriculture, Church planting and Health care (PREACH) program

Community Organizing and Development (CODE) Program

Projects

Food Always in the Home (FAITH) Gardening

Using Properly Lowland Integrated Farming Technology (UPLIFT)

Sloping Agricultural Land Technology (SALT 1)

Simple Agro-Livestock Technology (SALT 2)

Sustainable Agroforest Land Technology (SALT 3)

Small Agrofruit Livelihood Technology (SALT 4)

Seed production and plant propagation

Poultry, small animals and inland fish

Appendix 2
A look at the Magsaysay impact area

Location	Bila, San Miguel, Magsaysay, Davao del Surro
Project started	1990
Initial MBRLC contact	Rodrigo Calixtro/Harold Watson
Project developer	Jeff Palmer

Background

Bila is about 20 kilometers from the main MBRLC Center. It was considered a strategic impact area due to the number of lowlanders living in the marginal upland areas. The people here are characterized as lowlanders living in the uplands, well below the poverty level for the Philippines. They are subsistence farmers whose food staple is maize (corn).

The original contact was made from a displaced Baptist family who wanted a Bible study in their home. Mr. Rod Calixtro, farm manager of MBRLC, and Mr. Harold Watson, director of MBRLC, were the first to enter the area and conduct home Bible studies. However, due to the demands of work in other areas, the work was turned over to Mr. Jeff Palmer, another MBRLC staff member.

A Bible study was carried out through most of 1990 with the group growing from one to about six families. The method of teaching used was Chronological Bible Story Telling (CBST). As the group progressed through the Bible study, problems related to human suffering in the area were raised and discussed. As the group came together as a spiritual body, they also began talking and exploring possibilities of how to solve or alleviate the physical problems in the area such as chronic malnutrition and water shortages.

By the middle of 1991, the small group had organized into a church and formed a farmers' club among the members. As the church building was being put in place, many members were also "building" their farms by using technologies developed by the MBRLC. As the church grew in members and began to spread into neighboring *sitios*, the projects of the farmers and the farmers' club also expanded.

Results of the work

Today, the Magsaysay project has grown to a maturing impact area with multifaceted results. From the start of a Bible study in one home with one family, there are now three maturing churches along with two active

preaching points. In addition, there are another three villages in the immediate area calling out the Macedonian call of "come help us."

In terms of the theological education, the CBST approach has
helped to educate the local people in good, solid Bible knowledge and
equipped them with a firm foundation on which to build their Christian
beliefs. In addition, 13 local people have been trained and recently gradu-
ated from a seminary extension basic foundations course and another
three have been trained through the BOOST program of integrated agriculture, Bible study and health care.

In terms of physical development, from the one group of farmers
in the Bila church about 8 *sitios* are now partners in participation in community development programs. This area of participation extends about 7
kilometers along the face of the Alip mountain range, with the center of
the work being *sitio* Bila.

The original farmers' organization has expanded to include 14
families. They have all undertaken small scale agroforestry projects for the
development of their farms and food and income generation. They have
been the beneficiaries of an animal dispersal program in recognition of
their hard work. They also have worked to establish a spring development project with two outlets in strategic locations in their *sitio*. The club,
through cooperative effort, has purchased a purebred male goat and a
purebred breeding boar to in order to improve and upgrade the existing
animal gene pool in their area.

As the Bila Christian Farmer's Club expanded and work became
open in neighboring villages, the MBRLC initially hired a agriculture
extensionist to work in the general area. The new work also yielded good
results and in turn another agriculturist and one church planter/devel-
oper was hired to help facilitate the program in the area.

All along the way the local and area government officials have
taken an active role in the program. The MBRLC works with the Local
Government Units (LGUs) in their planning and development of upland
programs in the area. Moreover, officers of the Department of Agriculture
and other government employees are seen as team members in the work
in these areas and many times they can be seen working side by side with
the MBRLC extensionists.

Examples of changed lives

Juanito and Juanilla Juario have six children. Initially, they both were
Roman Catholic but nominal in their beliefs. Juanito was a drunkard and
abused of his wife. After receiving the gospel his life changed from an
abuser to a provider for his family. He now has improved his farm with

agroforestry, has gotten a job and holds it in good standing, and is a leader of the Bila church.

Ben Butaya was an animist and a follower of B'Laan tribal religion. His wife Rosita was nominal Roman Catholic. Rosita was converted first and received persecution at the hands of her husband. For one full year she prayed earnestly for him and her family. After that time, Ben came to the missionary and asked to be baptized. When questioned as to the fact as to why he needed to be baptized, Ben responded with a beautiful presentation of the gospel. Rolsita had put her prayers into action and been sharing all along what she was learning as a new Christian.

Ben is now the evangelist of the Bila church. He goes from door to door sharing the gospel in neighboring village. In fact, he helped start the Bacungun work, which now has a maturing church. Ben has overcome his drinking problem, he now owns a cow, purebred goat and has implemented agroforestry projects in all of his upland farms. He also became the head of a village group that facilitated a water system for their village with Ben and Rosita donating the land for the outlet.

Nestor and Susan Blantukas live about three kilometers from Bila and heard the gospel through the ministry of Bila Baptist Church. They then became some of the founding members of the Bacungan church. Nestor is illiterate but has improved his livelihood by adopting agroforestry models of the MBRLC. Also, he and Susan have entered into a private and semi-communal reforestation program and are looking forward to greater income generation in the next five years. Susan serves as Bible woman (teacher) for the young church, and Nestor is a recognized leader of the group.

Conclusion

The Magsaysay impact area is just one example of the work of the MBRLC and its extension programs that concentrate on holistic community development. From the start of a small home Bible study with one family in March 1990, the project has grown to three churches with two preaching points and a number of other possible preaching sites. In addition, the agriculture and economic conditions of the people in the area are continuing to steadily improve with the people themselves taking the lead in their community development.

4
A church emerging in rural Cambodia

Margot Sluka and Tri Budiardjo

D uring recent months, Cambodians spanning the range of the local social hierarchy in rural Oudong District publicly professed the sole lordship of Jesus Christ. They are planning a group baptism and the building of a local church. This is their dramatic story.

A health and development project stimulated the emergence of this church where none had previously existed (nor where Christians could be found). The Oudong Rural Health Project envisioned it, planted the seed and then facilitated the harvest.

Three elements set this project apart. The church resulted from development efforts rather than missions or church-planting work as traditionally understood. An unprecedented level of cooperation by foreign NGOs and national churches resulted. Finally, the new Christ group does not hinge on the leadership of a single charismatic leader (which renders Cambodian churches so vulnerable to failure); several leaders are being raised up at once.

This radical religious change or group conversion was unlikely to happen. It began with only one expatriate couple's vision, who moreover were not church planters but medical experts. This couple began their work with an entirely non-Christian, government-assigned field team and non-Christian office staff. The project must still operate in a somewhat hostile social and political environment. Finally, the project area is dominated by an ancient demonic stronghold of national significance.

Spiritual and cultural environment

Naga, the seven-headed serpent who showed favor to the Buddha, has been the real prince of Cambodia. His ubiquitous symbol adorns public places both civic and religious, and the country's architecture and other art. The Naga's primary ancient stronghold has been the fabled Angkor, the world's largest religious monument and one of the seven wonders of the world, hidden in the jungles of northwest Cambodia.

The Naga's second most important seat has been over Oudong Mountain, for 250 years the royal capital and home to particularly religious and politically beleaguered kings. This lone, pagoda-topped set of mountains is also tied to historical legends that give it further spiritual significance.

Cambodian society is still spiritually captive to the Prince of Darkness. The establishment of a Christ group at the foot of Oudong Mountain is perceived by national church leaders as a victory in the spiritual battle over territory in Cambodia. However, the church near Angkor is in great difficulty.[1]

Theravada Buddhism has been reinstated as the state religion. But Cambodia's religious context has always been syncretistic; its Buddhism presents atypical patterns in that it is tightly interwoven with ancient local animism and some Brahman-Hindu elements introduced in antiquity with Indian civilization. (In fact, Hinduism had been the state religion during part of the classic Angkor period.)

As with peasant societies elsewhere, traditional Cambodian society has been characterized by a perennial search for protection from threats to its security such as absolutist human rulers and elites, natural forces, and vindictive spirits. Cambodians have had a choice of countless gods and spirits that could be tried for efficacy, although this abundance may in turn have diffused strong belief in any one of them.

Despite the traditional centrality of religion, overt religious interest is much reduced today. Genocide, extermination of religious leadership, destruction of temples, and prolonged religious prohibition have left a spiritual vacuum.

Uninterrupted political crisis has resulted in a state of alienation that fosters the disintegration of social norms. Moreover, Buddhist philosophy, with its emphasis on accepting the earned circumstances of one's present reincarnation, is said to be inimical to economic development and other forms of progress. On all counts, there may be a sense that Buddhism has failed to save Cambodians.

Buddhist practices in the area served by the Oudong Rural Health Project (ORHP) are acknowledged to be very superficial, motivated mainly by loyalty to surviving elders and its connection to a renascent nationalism. By contrast, fear of local and ancestral spirits is more likely to affect day-to-day decisions.

When the project was initiated, the government had just lifted religious restrictions directed especially against Christianity, which was seen as a Western religion. (Before that, people could be jailed just for learning and speaking English.) Foreign humanitarian workers were spied on and expelled from the country if found engaged in so-called Christian activities. Cambodian Christians worshiped (and even sang) in whispers.

Despite a new religious freedom law and a general thawing of official attitudes, most Cambodians are still traumatized by the risks of the past and still fear that allegiance to the wrong group could end in personal disaster.[2] There is no easy counterweight for continued authoritarianism, pervasive government corruption, increasingly sharp economic inequalities in the city and unabated Khmer Rouge terror in the provinces.

Project history

As the 1990s began, a growing political openness in Cambodia allowed foreign organizations to work at the grassroots. Accordingly,

World Vision (WV) Cambodia reviewed and redefined the direction of its ministry. The guiding theme was Micah 4:2-7:

> Many nations will come and say, "Come, let us go up to the mountain of the LORD, to the house of the god of Jacob. He will teach us his ways, so that we may walk in his paths." The law will go out from Zion, the word of the LORD from Jerusalem. He will judge between many peoples and will settle disputes for strong nations far and wide. They will beat their swords into plowshares and their spears into pruning hooks. Nation will not take up sword against nation, nor will they train for war anymore. Every man will sit under his own vine and under his own fig tree, and no one will make them afraid, for the LORD Almighty has spoken.
>
> All the nations may walk in the name of their gods; we will walk in the name of the LORD our God for ever and ever. "In that day," declares the LORD, "I will gather the lame; I will assemble the exiles and those I have brought to grief. I will make the lame a remnant, those driven away a strong nation. The LORD will rule over them in Mount Zion from that day and forever."

WV Cambodia formulated a new country strategy, including a country-specific vision statement. The seed of holism was planted in the organization. The vision of community bearing the marks of the kingdom of God was introduced.

The Oudong District Hospital-based RINE (Rehydration, Immunization, Nutrition, and Education) center was subsequently phased out and in its stead a broader, community-based rural health project was initiated in July 1991. Preah Srae Commune"s infirmary was selected for an expanded project center site.

The project was started in partnership with the Ministry of Health, which made the project team a diverse mix of people. The first project manager, an Australian who held advanced degrees from a major Western medical institution, led a team of Cambodian Government staff from province through commune levels with minimal academic background as well as respected villagers with even less formal education. He was assisted by his British wife, a nurse-midwife. The second project manager, an Austrian citizen and a US resident, has a background in public health and anthropology.

This diversity, in fact, presented a wonderful opportunity for witness, as all were aware of formidable barriers to meaningful relationships, which required intention and purpose to overcome. The fruits of sincere and reciprocal relationship building (the first couple spoke good Khmer), witnessing through lifestyle, persistent sharing of the Good News, and faithful prayer are the foundation for holism in project team life and in its work with the communities of Preah Srae.

Preah Srae Commune has 18 villages and 6,135 people, made up of 1,059 families, roughly one-third of which are headed by women (i.e., are without adult male labor); average family size is six. The project center lies 3 kilometers west of Highway 5 and Oudong Market, which in turn lies 45 kilometers north of Phnom Penh.

Though *Preah Srae* means "ricefields of the king," soil fertility is very low. Households subsist on rice cultivation, but the average one hectare per family cannot satisfy food needs year-round. This has led to widespread indebtedness to local Chinese money lenders, who occupy the few tile-roof houses.

The primary source of cash derives from family-based palm sugar production during the dry season, though many have no palm trees. In fact, the sugar palm is a symbol of Cambodia, dotting the countryside and lining the rice paddies. Homes traditionally stand on "leg" posts; some homes are built of wood, some of palm tree leaves, but many only qualify as huts. Poor, sandy roads make transportation very difficult.

Household-based economic activities also include basket weaving and food-vending. However, 49.7 percent of the commune population was recorded in 1991 as being unable to work due to age or handicap.[3]

In these needy communities, the health project was developed according to communities' own agendas. It addressed the whole range of needs and problems perceived and prioritized by the people themselves.

The project has a strong community organization component, relatively open-ended plans and participative decision making. The people set the agenda in recognition that good health for the poor can be attained only by helping people improve their entire life situation. This responsiveness to locally felt needs has initially made for a heavy emphasis on development, but has increasingly produced a pattern of programs that is now about half health and half development activities:

Health programs include immunization and growth monitoring; family planning, including a mobile team to reach more distant villages; antenatal and postnatal care and other maternal and child health services; a village health volunteer program and traditional birth attendant program; essential drugs and supplies; first aid and treatment of endemic diseases; health and nutrition education in the villages and primary schools, with regular training and supervision for primary schoolteachers; supportive supervision of commune health workers district-wide; and production of appropriate health education literature.

Development programs include one development club per village (with five club executives each); a cash and a paddy credit program in each club, for income-generation and food security respectively; water and sanitation activities (wells, toilets, rainwater tanks, and treadle pumps); aquaculture (fish-raising) and domestic animals; veterinary activities; vegetable gardening; reforestation (mainly fruit trees); infrastructure building (schools, roads, ponds, dams, health centers); a Benevolent Fund and Case Work program (one-time relief for tragedies that befall the very poor; a short-term mentoring program).

Pairing off and grouping the government counterparts in a variety of ways (putting them in charge of certain villages and activity areas), makes for natural integration of health and development, and for project efficiency. The same individuals function as health care providers and health educators (they are nurses) as well as community development activists (a major philosophical commitment and personal interest of theirs).

Sustainability of the entire program depends in part on the sustainability of the village development clubs. Credit interest generates a modest income for its leadership (including village health workers). The "modeling at the project center" development activities (aimed at the education of project visitors) also provide actual income for the commune-level counterparts at their infirmary. This should allow them to serve future health and related needs.

At the heart of all project interventions has been a continuous emphasis on intensive training for empowerment. This central strategy has become the strength of the project and helps make project activities viable over the long run. Hands-on technical training for practical applications of topics aims at self-reliance. Even more important, especially at first, was intensive training directed at changes in perceptions, values, and behavior, explicitly built on biblical principles.

Shortly before the conversion events, a new project accountant and driver were hired; this soon proved to be the addition of the project "evangelists." Phany and Ravy had suffered greatly and been singled out for execution during the Pol Pot years, but were saved; both are living testimonies of God's providence, and project participants believe their hires to be providential.

Christ group formation

A series of unusual events culminated first in the Christian conversion of the entire work team. All government counterparts and staff both in the field and in the Phnom Penh office accepted the Lordship of Jesus Christ during their work, in small groups, over several months. Soon, paraprofessionals in the project area (such as schoolteachers and district health workers), then ordinary villagers with their leaders and elders and whole families also joined the movement. The growth of this Christ group occurred in an upward curve of accelerating momentum. Some highlights:

Encounters with Christian community

In encounters with Christian community, people saw Christianity demonstrated in real life and seriously inquired. A three-day project study visit (in April 1994) to WV Cambodia's Kompong Thom relief and development project in central Cambodia marked the beginning of the overt movement of Oudong Rural Health Project people toward Christ. The project manager had felt led to arrange for the visit when hearing of the outstanding motivation and Christian commitment of the national team there. She hoped that the ORHP counterparts, themselves hardworking and proud of it, might be humbled and recognize a better model in the Kompong Thom group.

Her hopes were far exceeded. On the pretext of preparing project questions for the next day, the women's group got her up late at night, and by candle light eventually accused her of not teaching them about the Bible and the True God—explicitly, not doing her job. She had been more culturally sensitive than spiritually bold until confronted by these Buddhist women, who thought the whole cultural sensitivity issue ridiculous.

In Kompong Thom, the counterparts were impressed by what made this group of development workers distinct—their strong faith and their Bible studies and devotions. The counterparts wanted what the WV workers had. The pressure was on to "supply" it quickly, as if it were just another training workshop or project activity.

Immediately on their return to their own project, the counterparts initiated their own morning devotions along the model they had observed, supplementing the prayers they had said over their meals. Grappling with this new activity and the Bibles, music, and study materials such as Living Water, they opened in prayer, sang, and studied Scripture (perhaps with limited understanding).

In June 1994, three counterparts and four WV staff undertook a day-trip to a commune on the Southern end of Oudong District, ostensibly to assess damages to the commune infirmary just burned to the ground by Khmer Rouge guerillas. In reality, it provided a timely excuse to visit the district's only church, located in a village next to the burned infirmary.

Providentially, two Malaysian lay-missionary couples were holding a revival meeting in that isolated, rural church. Led there by God from Malaysia in a dream, they camped out on the straw mats covering the church floor for four days, in marathon sessions of prayer, praise, teaching and healing. They immediately took charge of our group on arrival. The astonished Cambodian villagers enjoyed the odd commotion and said they were impressed that God would bring such high-level visitors to minister to them. Brother Sar Paulerk, the missionaries' assistant, taught the entire Cambodian ORHP group—three counterparts and three staff—in the adjacent open shed while driver Ravy stood by in prayer. Each of the six made a commitment to Christ after hearing Br. Paulerk's clear and compelling exposition of the gospel.

Many hours later we were still in the sanctuary, hands raised high in worship, being noisily prayed over, pressed to speak in tongues and slain in the spirit. This was somewhat more than the worried project manager had bargained for. Barely remembering to leave the emergency medical supplies for the two communes, we returned long after curfew. Still reeling from the day's strange events, the new Christians said their hearts were full of gladness and peace.

Encounters with Christianity through teaching

After encountering Christianity through teaching, people responded by professing Christ as Lord. The two pillars of the Cambodian church, Brothers Barnabas and Paulerk,[4] alternately came for evangelistic outreach to the project, and at each visit a number of people professed Christ as Lord due to their powerfully clear and culturally relevant expositions; many others made private confessions. God first convicted Barnabas' wife to be a partner in her husband's ministry again, then to have a ministry of her own with women in the project area. She now accompanies the project team to Preah Srae as a representative of the national church.

In July 1994, Brother Paulerk and a Cambodian pastor's ministry at the project led five different people to accept the Lord in one day, following Bible teaching sessions and assigned reflection times. Kim San, team leader of WV's adjacent agriculture project was generally known as contrary and uncooperative, and opposed the sharing of the Good News for several years and drove Christian witness underground in his own project. An independent thinker and nonconformist, he spent many years in and around Buddhist monasteries. All present that Saturday benefited from his challenging questions. When he smilingly broke the news of his new birth to his weary superiors the following Monday morning, we were surprised to hear loud rejoicing coming from the agriculture office. A Saul had become a Paul.

Miing ("Aunt") Thon, the project center cook, is a poor, small but strong woman with many dependents and no formal education. She accepted the Lord the same day and now attends project meetings to learn new things after her kitchen tasks are done. So shy when first hired that she hid from expatriate staff, she has increasingly become a member of the team, and quite assertive in a playful way. She proudly replied to the project manager's teasing probe the following week: "I decided to become a Christian. And nobody made me."

One day in August, 35 people waited for Barnabas and his wife at the project center, and to the "old" Christians present, ten more were added, including a woman high school teacher, the woman in charge of the district MCH center, and the wives of two primary schoolteachers. (Unfortunately, many who had expressed interest could not spend time away from their rice fields in this ploughing and transplanting season.)

Inevitably, more people were found later to have made private decisions for Christ. When the project manager next discussed business with the field supervisor, he casually indicated that Mol Meak was "ready now" and asked her, after a pause, to "do it." After all staff and counterparts had solemnly gathered around the long table in the center, it was found that in fact three more counterparts were poised to officially give over their lives to Jesus Christ (leaving now only Som Ouen). All rose, the assistant manager translated a long version of the sinner's prayer, then driver Ravy prayed at length over each of the three, and each one in turn prayed for whatever had been left out.

When asked later (at their "God-accepting celebration" with cookies and tea under the big bamboo), just when they had arrived at this decision in their hearts, they conceded it was the previous Saturday at the big teach-in. They had been too shy to come forward with so many outsiders present because outsiders already considered all ORHP counterparts to be Christians.

At WV Cambodia's Annual Staff Retreat in September, the last of the ten ORHP counterparts officially became part of the project family of faith; Nyoung Som Ouen came forward on the last day. He had held out that long because of loyalty to his spirit-medium mother, a very important elder in his village, whose censure he feared. Now 100 percent of our field workers had professed Christ, in addition to other paraprofessionals in the area through whom ORHP works, and the others had matured at this retreat. Returning to the project elated, counterpart Ly Ngan spoke of the Holy Spirit as one would about an old, well-known friend.

Encounters with God's spiritual power

In this kind of encounter, people experienced the superior supernatural reality of God and commited themselves fully to Christ. A successful exorcism, a spontaneous confrontation of the powers created a spark that crossed from the project center to the villages.

Project area villagers are extremely poor and beset by practical problems and struggles for day-to-day survival. They seek concrete help, not doctrine or promises. Such an answer came in the form of superior, problem-solving spiritual power when they were desperate and at the end of their wisdom and resources. This power generated the spark to reach the ordinary rural people—who are, after all, the intended project beneficiaries.

A distraught husband, accompanied by relatives, brought his wife Phun from a nearby village to the project center infirmary. They and others unanimously diagnosed her as demon possessed, and asked the project counterparts to pray over her. In the name of Jesus, they talked with the evil spirit within her, who replied at one point: "I know Jesus, but he is not my god; he was my student." After concerted prayer efforts over her, she returned to normal. Later at home, however, she again became possessed.

Project accountant Phany and project driver Ravy had been asked to come to the project center to join the prayer efforts for Phun. Phany proceeded to talk with her, or rather the spirit within her, to orient herself to the reality at hand, to "test the spirit." At her question "Do you know me?" she received cruel glares, contorted face, bulging eyes ("like in a Dracula movie"), then Phun panicked, violently throwing off Phany's hand.

Phany then offered the desperate husband all she had: "I can pray for her in Jesus' name, but I have no magic." He was eager to do anything to get her well; all else they could think to try had failed and they were at their wits' end.

Meanwhile Phun had managed her escape home to the village, where she could not be persuaded to return by the relative sent for her. So the waiting, hungry counterparts, long returned from work in the villages, ate lunch, while Phany and Ravy went off to fast and pray instead.

After Phun was finally forcibly hauled back by her husband and counterpart Thy, extended dialogue ensued between Phany and the "ghost," with the wide-eyed counterparts in attendance. Phany was very strict with the spirit over its evasions and lies, but heard Phun say that "the big teacher over there ordered me to go into her, so I must obey; . . . but I have not come to live permanently in her." The spirit claimed to be alone in her body, and claimed to be yet unnamed.

At Phany's strict admonition to "speak clearly" (the spirit had been speaking in a barely audible, unclear, female voice), "she" finally admitted that God is bigger than ghosts, first having claimed the opposite. Reminding the spirit of its fears, and on the supreme authority of Jesus, Phany persuaded Phun to take off the hidden magic string across her waist. (Such a string is very common protection against witches in Cambodia, discovered even on

WV staff; it consists of a nylon string with a lead plate inscribed with magic formula). At first, Phun refused, saying "The teacher will cause me trouble." After many authoritative commands in the name of "God, who you say is bigger," Phun untied it and handed it to Phany, who prayed over it and then flushed it down the project's toilet.

The moment Phun surrendered her magic string, her face, eyes, and behavior suddenly returned to normal, and she became extremely weak (previously, even two or three people could not control her). Before and after the string was removed, Phany reminded Satan of all the reasons why he had no right to invade this woman. Phany said, "You already know where to go [the abyss], now you go under the foundation of the cross of Jesus."

Phun said, "Now I feel relief because everything is taken out from my body; it seems that somebody left my body . . . I no longer hear voices speaking in my ear."

Phany: "Who is speaking to me now?"

"Phun."

"Phun or no-name person speaking?" Phany asked.

"Phun."

During the prayer that followed, all became calm. Her husband accepted Jesus as Lord of his life, as he had promised, as did Phun herself, "since my husband accepts." Prayer and much instruction on how to pray and behave now followed. They were told, "God doesn't want your incense and idols and food offerings" and instructed about the need for regular confession of sins and reconciliation with all people in their lives. (Phun later kneeled on both knees before the astonished project cook, her aunt, begging forgiveness: "I treated you wildly because of the spirit; it was not me.")

When Phany and Ravy returned from Phnom Penh for follow-up, both Phun and her husband smiled and welcomed them on arrival—all was still well. She affirmed she knew that now her body belonged to her. She was asked, "Who is it?" and replied, "Phun," laughing at the question.

Her husband updated Phany on her condition, saying with emotion that she now spoke politely and softly with him, even invited him to eat with her, and treated the babies gently. She began to eat a lot; previously she had accepted only one or two spoonfuls, refusing even water, and still physically overpowered several others. Phany reminded both of them of the spiritual truths they had learned the previous day and their new spiritual commitment. After the counterparts returned from their work in the villages, they all spent time in prayer and instruction.

The next day was again troubled. The counterpart, Som Ouen came late to the project center at 8:00 a.m., as he was busy "ploughing for his wife." Since his physical diagnosis of Phun was malnutrition and weakness from extreme poverty, he set off to buy "medicine" (a glucose-vitamin I.V. solution) for her at Oudong market. However, in his absence Phun became uncontrollable again and caused her husband and the counterparts much trouble. So Yan and Chet Em told Ouen on his return "she fears only you."

On September 30, Ouen prayed by the project center gate, blocking it with prayer, asking God to prevent Satan from taking Phun back out. He heard God saying in a clearly audible voice not to worry, that someone had already "worked for her."

Ouen remembered that all WV staff were in the annual Day of Prayer (marking the end of fiscal year 1994), and he reassured her fearful Buddhist *Achar* (lay-teacher) father that he felt Phany and Ravy had already interceded for her. Indeed they had at that very time—at 9:45 a.m. and at every subsequent prayer session. Ouen's mention of current spiritual struggle caused the devout *Achar* father to fear even more and offer to borrow more money to help her "sickness," as poor and indebted as he already was.

Worsening events began to greatly worry Ouen, and around 4:00 p.m., again at the project gate, God's clear, loud voice enjoined him: "Help them, help them," so that he went off again to Oudong market to buy more "medicine" (vitamins) and food. Phun then steadily improved, and even invited Ouen to join her for the special soup he had bought her.

The following evening, Ouen came from his nearby village to the project center to begin his guard duty at 6:00 p.m. After praying for Phun in the infirmary, he retreated to pray by himself before retiring on the long table of the center.

Ouen was awakened at 12 midnight. He heard the loud, clear, voice of God admonishing him. "You did not pray for her correctly . . . you just keep praying for her but do not teach her nor her husband to pray for themselves." Following two sleepless hours, God also led him to copy some instructions for the husband from the hymn book, including the Ten Commandments. (The next morning, the husband regretted that Ouen had not awakened him in turn.)

Phun had dabbled in all kinds of religions for a long time, trying them all, dividing up the floor space in her house among her various spirits, beckoning them down the center post of her house, conversing with them, increasingly frightening those around her. The project manager felt that the despair of extreme poverty propelled her toward the only hope or promises of help she knew. Confrontation with Phun's plight will accelerate the project's efforts to reach the "poorest of the poor" with adjustments to its current programs and with innovations. It also underlines the importance of a whole gospel to these villagers so marginal in survival terms, a gospel which also feeds, clothes, houses, and heals.

Meanwhile God had begun, through this unusual episode, to single out for overriding spiritual leadership Nyoung Som Ouen—the last counterpart to go public. He has emerged as a remarkable man of prayer, faith, obedience, decisiveness, and independence from others' opinions and social pressures. (Ironically, family concerns had kept him underground the longest.) His history of supernatural experiences before and after conversion confirms God's choice. Counterparts Ly Ngan and Hong Thy have also emerged as Christian leaders through their witnessing activities and their hunger for insight into God's Word.

On October 14, despite only one evening's notice, forty people awaited Barnabas, his wife, Phany and Ravy, including some community leaders who happened to come by for business that morning and ended up staying the day.

Barnabas taught the morning session on the question of which god to worship (comparing religions and gods of other countries to the True God). The afternoon session taught how to worship God ("frankly, truly"), and included the story of Satan. He relied much on Scripture, and pointed to God's power as opposed to ours, power that depends on the blood of Jesus.

Barnabas concluded each session by asking "Is it true or not?" The villagers replied in unison: "That's true!"

"When we accept God, He will stay with us!" Phany was stunned at this spontaneous statement by the Buddhist *Achar*, words that she attributes to the inspiration of the Holy Spirit in him. Even after viewing several challenging videos midday, there were still no questions: "It's all true, so we have no questions!" This teaching day was unique in that alone.

Barnabas concluded with an invitation, "If you think this is the real story, do you want to accept God?" Three women stood up—the wives of counterparts Som Ouen, Khem How and Hong Thy—and were prayed over by the group.

Hong Thy rose next to convey that two people wished Barnabas to cast spirits from their bodies. Two more women rose: Som Ouen's 68-year-old mother Jenn, a spirit-medium and healer, and his 48-year-old sister Kang, also a spirit-medium and one of the project's traditional birth attendants. (Phany began weeping and Som Ouen became most teary-eyed; he had longed for years that the women he loved would abandon the spirits to keep them from passing to the next generation.) Both answered that a lot of spirits lived inside them, and Barnabas carefully noted their names on paper. He sent these spirits to the desert, far away from any human beings, and helped the women to accept Christ.

The old healer asked also for the cleansing of her house: "Please come and take all the worship things out." At this point, Barnabas quietly predicted that there would come to be more Christians there.

As all were leaving, the Tuol Sophy *Achar* again affirmed the truth of the day's teaching. (He and other men had determined to stay only briefly but ended up staying the day.) Phun's ten-year-old daughter also came to Christ that day.

As requested, Barnabas, his wife, Phany and Ravy then went to the old healer's house in Srae Chenda village. The rickety palm-leaf structure next to her son Ouen's small house shared a compound with many residents. Barnabas first called all the young children of the extended household onto the bamboo bed under Ouen's house, where they were prayed over for protection and dedication. Five neighbors silently regarded the whole scene.

Finally, the old healer's youngest daughter and a granddaughter (the one who was chosen to carry forward the healer role into the next generation) surrendered their magic strings to Barnabas and climbed up to the old grandmother's house. Because she is frail, she only pointed out what she wanted removed, and Barnabas, Phany, and Ravy made a pile of her paraphernalia downstairs. Barnabas prayed over the pile, then asked Ouen for fire. Ouen lit it, while his old mother quickly made her way back upstairs for a few magic cloths and magic strings that had been forgotten. Barnabas then read aloud the list of about ten spirits recorded earlier at the project center (some have the names of weapons, some names relate to ancient myths), and he addressed the spirits: "Jenn and Kang no longer need you now, because they accept God," then burned the list. The neighbors were still silently watching the unprecedented events.

The team returned to Phnom Penh at 7:00 p.m. The project area now had its first whole Christian family, and a three- to four-generation family no less. (Ravy, who knows the Cambodian church scene, remarked the next day that this was the first whole Christian family he had ever heard of in Cambodia—"There is always someone missing, parents, or children, or a spouse.") Following her conversion, the old matriarch expressed grief at the unsaved status of faraway family members.

As the above events were recounted and translated in the usual convoluted, time-consuming way and recorded in the office, Dr. An exclaimed: "I think that all the neighbors now will wait to see what happens to that family! Because this means a very big attitude change, which is always difficult and never easy, so it amazes people! If the family is successful and unharmed, I think people must follow her again, because before people also followed her with the spirits!" She added "God knows the importance of the family, and that Ouen and his family are one and the same! Religion is important to social transformation."

Sequelae and analyses

Counterparts had seemed slow to involve their wives, but they joined readily. Women defer to their husbands, especially in public decisions. (Cambodian women are particularly vulnerable now as their numbers exceed men's, which contributes to highly unstable marriages in the project area and license by husbands. Even in the villages prostitution is rife, and desertions are common).

Som Ouen immediately began a tradition of daily family devotions. After nightfall (when he used to sleep), the extended family inside his palm-leaf house now sings and praises God for two hours; the neighbors now ask them what this new worship is all about. (Right across the road, fence posts display white drawings to frighten off disease-causing spirits—dengue hemorrhagic fever, for example, is causing deaths in this village.) Som Ouen is intent on building up his large family first. His daily Bible studies are directed at the children; the large old blackboard leaning against the cardboard walls of his home now displays the Lord's Prayer (in its Khmer hymn-form). Khem How had similarly begun daily family devotions (his ten-year-old already loves reading the Bible) and reaching out to other relatives.

As developments unfold, they increasingly bear the marks of classic group conversion. Until now the closed little Christian group was based on occupational and work affiliation and physical proximity. (The counterparts had been particularly tightly knit. Because they also eat and live together most of the week, loyalty and bonds of trust and friendship developed from the start.)

Now increasingly there is also a Christ group on the basis of nuclear- and extended-family ties in the villages, which makes for stability and roots (that is, sustainability). Som Ouen, had right after his family's conversion gone house to house after dark to tell his fellow-villagers of Jesus Christ. Some just listened to him; others asked questions.

The field supervisor remarked, "We are not only talking to our own families. We already talk to all the people in the villages as part of our work." One day, while he was attending to school construction business, the Tuol Sophy *Achar* and twenty workers questioned him at length about the dramatic events at the project center and asked to be included next time a Christian teacher came. According to counterpart Ly Ngan, some village health volunteers had also said they wanted to attend the next teaching session. Work relationships were immediately used as a vehicle for witness.

In fact, the new Christians had immediately addressed the leadership problem following their public confessions, and (with wisdom born, no doubt, from bitter experience) had notified both political and religious leaders of it, undercutting possible opposition. Ly Ngan had notified the Oudong District Hospital director (her work superior and former nemesis) and the District Governor. In fact, administration and health authorities later came looking for her to ask why she had become a Christian. Som Ouen notified the commune leader of his decision. The authorities were even invited to future teaching sessions on Christianity. If any opposition can be said to exist at all right now, it is muted.

Fearlessness is not their only visible fruit of the Spirit, but it is remarkable after a lifelong history of vicious repression and uncharacteristic of the Khmers, so long conditioned into passive compliance and self-protection. Jenn and Kang had both greatly feared retaliation from the evil spirits when they ventured forth to hear Barnabas. Now they no longer fear at all, they say, and they feel much healthier and stronger physically.

Meak and his brother Touch had slept in the rice fields and by the project chicken house late August for fear of kidnaping by the Khmer Rouge. Meak now prays, and fears just a little, he says.

Other signs of change are also noticeable in their character. For instance, they are more truthful, trying to save face with God now rather than with their fellows.

God seems to combat cultural weaknesses with cultural strengths, dealing with new Christians in ways they recognize or expect. Grandmother Jenn, the old healer, had two dreams the Sunday night following her conversion. In the first dream, she went into a pond to cut two lotus flowers, when a leech latched onto her leg. She succeeded only after much pulling to pull first half of it off, finally the rest. The leech, she said, represented the evil spirits, sucking out her life. The first half came off at her conversion; the second half came off when she had her spirit paraphernalia burned.

In the second dream she dreamed that she was choking on a fish bone (again representing the evil spirits in her); when she cried out to God to save her, it was expelled. These dreams are easily interpreted by the whole happy, laughing family. The old healer then raised her folded hands high above her head and repeated: "Thank you, Jesus! Thank you, God!"

What a humbling privilege it has been these weeks to watch up close the great theater of God's works, and at times to participate at the margins.

Opposition

On the second day of the annual WV Cambodia Retreat, a severely shaken Phany confided that the previous day, "Satan tried to attack my family." Her 12-year-old daughter was kidnaped for selling into prostitution. She was drugged and taken from one place to another all over Phnom Penh for bargaining over.

The story had quite a miraculous ending several hours later. In an alley on the southwestern boundary of the city, the girl briefly came out of her drugged state to recognize the back of her aunt's house (the only relative in town). She broke through the fence and under the traditional house (on pillar posts) and cried for help. Her father was subsequently fetched from a ministry; her abductors had fled. (She was back in her drug-induced state for a few more days.) The family continued to fear for several days as a strange man watched the home in the parents' absence, but when he disappeared, anxiety gave way to great thanksgiving and rejoicing for the child's unlikely rescue.

Immediately after this, Phany was instrumental in the successful exorcism at the project center. God then roused her several times on the brink of sleep, startling her non-Christian husband, and entreating her, "Please, pray for Phun."

During the same week that most listeners responded to the gospel, a struggle of different sorts for the project unfolded at the Phnom Penh office. A funding agency liaison person visited the project and, seeing Bibles there, warned of instant loss of funding, given that ORHP is a health and development project funded from public sources. The alarmed project manager inadvertently frightened the counterparts. At the same time, great work pressures kept the project manager from paying due attention to the unusual developments in the field. Tight deadlines for a third version of a project proposal culminated in the decision by management not to submit it. This left the project temporarily without a funding source. In fact, all along, facilitating expatriate staff had encountered adversity of their own, such as lingering illness, and midnightly frights, while new Christians were being born in the field.

The evening before the August 1994 outreach Barnabas had expressed much excitement because of God's clear direction for it, but was sorely afflicted, sick, and without sleep. When Ravy drove up early morning, Barnabas said he suddenly felt fine.

Ripple effect on project effectiveness

This testimony must also acknowledge other inevitable, spin-off changes affecting people's lives in the larger project area. Since cultural elements are interconnected, a profound change in world view and values also affect other domains.

The project has become more effective because the counterparts have more patience and compassion regarding the villagers. The increase in motivation, vision, and concern for the people has meant improvements in team cohesion, planning for the future, problem-solving (e.g., for rural credit), and teaching of health and development principles and goals. These things take on deeper meaning now; counterparts have begun to think of the villagers in eternal terms.

There are more inquirers from the villages. The development club leader of Svay Pok village was interested in Christianity because "it is the Christians who are genuinely interested in helping the poor." The field supervisor's English teacher was interested after watching the Christians help one another. According to Som Ouen, Srae Chenda villagers' interest goes back to Doug and Sally's time because of their unselfishness and the way they used to hug the very dirty boys, treating them like important people.

Prey Phdiak and Tuol Pong Ro were old problem villages, isolated and perhaps the Commune's poorest, with a reputation for drinking, gambling, wife-beating, and related social problems. After a marked turnaround, Prey Phdiak and Tuol Pong Ro now have clubs on a par with other villages (one club accountant there is known for his meticulous, reliable work). Their inhabitants now relate to the project counterparts with trust, and are pressing the project to build a primary school. Impatient with funding process, they began to have their children instructed on reed mats in a private home lent to the cause. "We see now how the children of other villages can read and write, while ours are ashamed. Even our club leaders have trouble keeping up with their record-keeping and reporting." Vices are reduced to about one-third of previous levels. Villagers have begun to see themselves with a new perspective, comparing themselves and their clubs to those of other villages, and no longer accept their lesser status.

People are responding to the gospel and showing improvement in various aspects of their lives. The signs of the presence of the kingdom as described in Micah 4 generally, and in Isaiah 65 specifically have begun to become the experience of these people and their spirits are more receptive to God's Word.

Integration in this project no longer involves just health and development with a Christian witness component; rather, it means integration of all project activities with a growing understanding of their redemptive purpose. Counterparts have intuitively realized the connection between Christ's restoring work in their souls with that of their social and physical environment.

ORHP thus represents holistic ministry. It is not implemented by expatriates, but by excited new Christians; a holistic world view is their heritage. Their lives have not been fragmented by modern life, nor do they share expatriates' struggles for wholeness. More than once they have stunned (if not shamed) the expatriate project manager with the strength of their new convictions. Confronted with their matter-of-fact faith, she is more aware of some deeply rooted secularism within herself. By contrast, they are a worship-oriented people. In fact, the new Christians now minister to the expatriate project manager.

Ultimately, of course, holistic development is not the result of human social engineering (even with God's Word as foundation and framework). The outworking of God's spiritual power brings forth the experience of the kingdom in daily life situations; all aspects of life are redeemed, restored, and renewed. This is beyond proper project design, appropriate development strategy, and sincere humanitarian intentions. Only God's supernatural intervention in human efforts can bring forth that kingdom experience.

Factors contributing to church emergence

Biblical considerations

Counterparts and community were exposed to Christianity in work, word and wonder—a trinity for wholeness.

- Exposure to Christian community through *work*. Through the sacrificial living of the first project manager couple and the study trip to the Kompong Thom program, ORHP team members were exposed to Christianity in action. They were moved by the dedication of the newly Christian staff to the project work and to one other.

- Exposure to God's *word*. Constant witness from certain Christian project staff culminated in the Kraing Chek group conversion. Subsequent project visits of two national church leaders provided for intensive exposition of the Word in relevant ways that satisfied the quest of hardworking village women like Mol Thon and confrontive intellectuals like Kim San.

- Exposure to spiritual encounter or *wonder*. Holism is not only about the physical and spiritual aspects of human life. It also includes supernatural reality, which is necessary for human existence whether acknowledged or not. The dust of the earth and breath of God merged by the miraculous act of God. Here, good *work* and God's *word* similarly blended in holism by the miraculous intervention of God.

Project communities understand and live out the reality of supernatural intervention and interaction, such as the exorcism of a demon from Phun, the casting out of spirits from their mediums Jenn and Kang, and preventing generational spirits from being inherited again in their family. Acknowledgment that God is only a prayer away is an integral part of their new faith. One scriptural theme that appealed to them most powerfully was the Spirit's continued presence with them. (They had sought recourse to spirits in the first place because the Buddha was beyond their reach and control.) The True God must be real in that immediate spiritual realm. God is not only God of the body (physical reality) and the heart (inner world of the human) but is also God of the spiritual world.

Finally, all actors in the drama of this group conversion believe that it was directed or choreographed by God himself. He orchestrated it from the pre-project phase, as emphasized in the written testimonies of counterparts and staff (Ouen, An, Phany, Ravy, and others). The primacy of God's activity is acknowledged by World Vision International, as reflected in its mission statement.

Organizational analysis

Organization's commitment

The Mission Statement of the World Vision Partnership and the Vision Statement of WVI-Cambodia affirm the approach of the Oudong Rural Health Project. The aim is to ensure people's dignity through both an overall improved living standard or quality of life and opportunity to respond to the gospel.

In the absence of exact operational guidelines, there is freedom to explore methods for effective ministry in each individual project. The main catalyst for this exploration in WV Cambodia is the field ministries manager, who seeks to foster holistic project ministry increasingly in line with the organization's mission and vision statements and related commitments.

Opportunities for new behavior patterns and traditions to evolve

For a Christian organization like World Vision there are many legitimate, natural, non-threatening activities that provide forums for discussion and opportunities for the expression of deep meanings in the Christian life. The organizational annual retreat has been a milestone for many staff, some of whom openly professed their faith much later. Celebrating Christmas together and explaining the meaning of Easter are further examples.

In ORHP, prayer before the communal meals provided opportunities to verbalize the Christian faith. The project manager has always marveled at the ease with which non-Christian Cambodians can pray at considerable length (giving flies and other eager creatures ample access to the food). At the project center, praying aloud before meals naturally opened ways for brief devotions or discussions after meals.

Interpersonal analysis

Balanced Focus on Community and Individual

While God's concern is for community in Scripture (cf. Israel and the church), it does not come at the expense of the individual.

71

Holistic development must clearly focus on communities; benefit to individuals at the expense of the group is a hallmark of project failure. But ministry differs from development in also perceiving the importance of individuals. This provides the foundation for case work in the holistic development context.

ORHP had felt compelled to begin such a program focusing on individual development, because the poorest of the poor, their minds fully on present survival, tended to fall through the cracks of its systems and remained beyond the reach of credit schemes, pond digging campaigns, and health education sessions.

In the spiritual realm, Christian faith requires an individual decision and God seeks to raise individuals as leaders. At the same time, the counterparts' testimony is of a group conversion with a social context. Project staff were consciously embodying a caring community, showing Christian compassion, and communicating the dignity of the marginalized in the villages.

The exorcism story shows that the counterparts were quickly known and respected as Christians. Their private faith decisions immediately had an impact on others' decisions. Neither did their individual commitments come as a surprise to the community.

Dynamics at project level; obeying specific callings

The project was designed with people as the focus. Relationship building was given much attention, especially regarding the government counterparts. Expatriate staff invested their expertise, experience, and vision in the counterparts through genuine friendship. In the project, people matter most; they are above any other success indicators.

The people in whom the first project manager couple invested are living out the couple's vision, which is being reinforced and facilitated by the second project manager. She tried to follow the couple's pattern and enrich it with intentional gender awareness as part of a vision of community life which further reflects kingdom reality. Women were empowered under her leadership; she added three strong women to the team (two WV staff, and one counterpart). It is no wonder that the first group pressing for Bible teaching and knowledge of the True God consisted exclusively of women, and that the first group accepting the Lord were five women—four women counterparts and Dr. An—and one man. Women were the initial critical mass and pulled the men along with their urgent inquiries.

Strong friendship was fostered initially among the counterparts; this later provided a safe environment of acceptance despite differing convictions. This group dynamic served as a support system for those who made a decision for Christ and for those who had not yet done so. There was no pressure on either group to conform, no split or division, and day-to-day work continued in the same high team spirit. But the added joy of individuals who found new life colored the atmosphere of the team.

The continuity of God's work through different people in various stages of the project is reflected in a passage in Psalm 126:

> Those who sow tears shall reap joy. Yes, they go out weeping, carrying seed for sowing, and return singing, carrying their sheaves (Psalm 126:5-6, TLB).

All individuals contributing to the present movement of people toward Christ have demonstrated consistent obedience to various calls and roles that God assigned to them. Daily, intensive intercession and specific prayer have come from those who were given the burden to pray.

The first project manager couple, who jointly initiated ORHP and quietly nurtured the vision of a church there, faithfully prayed daily for the project workers long after their service in Cambodia had ended. For example, the second project manager alerted them by fax of the urgent need for a special prayer effort (a number of counterparts had expressed overt interest in the Bible and God's Spirit was moving tangibly and pressing for action). The couple quickly raised more than 50 prayer partners abroad.

Faithful witnessing was consistently carried out by those with language and cultural understanding. One villager said, "Sally was always sharing a Bible verse with us first." Upon request, Bibles, literature, hymnals, songsheets, study-guides, cassettes were taken to the field. Most recently obedience has come to mean merely inviting national leaders to teach, and to make linkages with other resource persons to facilitate that harvest.

Personal investment (including prayer and faithfulness in many small callings) seemed to be the overriding human factor in moving from a group of co-laborers and friends, to a devotion-group, to a spontaneous Christ group still struggling to define itself.

Counterparts have been pressing for group baptism and planning church construction. Quiet plans by Barnabas and Paulerk call for the baptism of selected leaders in the morning, who would then baptize the remainder in the afternoon. This allows for handing over church authority and official leadership and avoiding undue dependence on outsiders and other churches.

It is hoped that the new Christ group will then build a simple structure in village pagoda style, free of Western influences, mats covering the floor, thus truly welcoming of village residents. So far, everyone envisions a truly indigenous church springing up, relevant and vibrant, from its sociocultural context,

Factors hindering church emergence

Guiding principles have emerged for implementing a development project that leads to the formation of a Christ group or church, in contrast to a mission-based church-planting effort using development strategies.

Methodology vs. ministry of the Holy Spirit

The emergence of the Christ group within Oudong Rural Health Project is in fact not the result of appropriate strategy or methodology for Christian witness or of integrating specific components of holistic ministry in a project. God himself engineered unusual circumstances, honored the desires of his people, and worked at various levels of the ministry by moving different people to do different things. All of this, after a period of investment, led people in rapid succession to make decisions for Christ.

Practitioners in the development business are tempted to put more emphasis on well-developed strategy, sound methodology, and indicators of success than on God's sovereignty. The important strategy is to recognize that the Holy Spirit is there to make Christ known before the project does.

Professionalism vs. people-focused ministry

Today's demand is for professionalism in any vocational field, including Christian service. Professionalism gives assurance of quality and success. This poses different dilemmas to various levels of development people.

For the practitioners in the field, the problem is in the pressure to pursue all the academic and technical requirements of the work at the expense of focusing on people and building relationships, or even using the people served to achieve project goals instead of their own. In choosing a consultant, for example, the temptation is to neglect the people for whom the project was intended and look for a highly qualified professional backed by a prestigious agency to ensure a highly credible report and improve funding prospects.

For management this poses a dilemma in recruiting personnel. The temptation is to put qualifications and credentials above a call and commitment to the ministry. Had ORHP focused solely on professional-standard performance, a Christ group may not have emerged.

Human responsibility vs. divine calling

It is critical in the decision-making process at project level to select a strategy, mode of operation, or method of intervention with the goal of enabling people to discover the kingdom of God, along with or even above technical and managerial considerations. This is a personal decision but has eternal implications that may facilitate or hinder the ministry in a particular project.

Like any other so-called noble work, development can be inspired by humanitarian aspirations only or by divine calling. Development work (no matter how holistic it is) is easily perceived as human effort and professional vocation, compared to church planting or evangelism. It is easier to rally prayer support for evangelistic campaigns than for digging wells, organizing rice banks or conducting training in fish raising, despite their inherent spiritual dimension. It is very easy to forget that development work is a spiritual calling and ministry.

Project design

Proposal writing is a science and an art. It is a science in that the design must follow a sound theoretical base or framework. It is an art in that a project deals mainly in people. Above all, its people focus requires a project design to be spiritual ministry. It is a process of looking at the complete human reality, followed by questions about God's role and plans for it in the particular setting.

However, it poses a problem to practitioners when holism is the ultimate purpose of a ministry. How should the spiritual component of the project design be operationalized? Reality seems to conflict. There is built-in tension between project design and ministry intention. A project is by nature time-bound and has specific objectives to achieve. By contrast, ministry cannot be thus scheduled (Who could develop a development logframe model for Holy Spirit interventions?). Ministry must address issues that arise spontaneously (although there is one ultimate objective—the lordship of Christ acknowledged).

For management or organizational purposes, it is difficult to hold project managers and staff to tasks beyond the clearly specified objectives of the design. The temptation is not to hold people accountable for lack of results beyond specific objectives as accountability weakens in this area, the focus of the ministry shifts to tangibles instead of transformed lives.

Organizational climate

The largest human obstacle that may have retarded the progress of the spiritual ministry in the project was lack of concrete support and backup when most needed. The organization aspires to holistic ministry, but it does not prepare for appropriate response. Responses are left to those directly involved in the events.

The organization's vision is to enable Cambodians to discover the kingdom of God. But it is disturbing to discover that the organization does not know what to do, as though caught by surprise that people would respond to the gospel so soon. Support mechanisms at this point are lacking.

In fact, these are not even high-priority issues when people in many project areas are already turning to Christ, compared to other organization agendas such as developing strategies for integration, the district planning approach, ministry standards—all of which, ironically, are to enable people to discover the kingdom of God.

Toward more effective holistic ministry

Holistic ministry is a corporate effort because it is about relationships. Not only at the interface between project and community does the ministry team have to work with one vision. But also the line and support functions must be in tune with the vision and strategy for holistic ministry.

For any single project, this poses enormous challenges to the ministry team. ORHP is only one small project among WV Cambodia's 20 projects (in budget 3 percent of the total operation, in staff 2.5 percent). WV Cambodia is one of the largest NGOs in Cambodia and is part of the vast World Vision International Partnership, which operates in over 90 countries.

WV Cambodia had formulated its ministry direction based on Micah 4. It has helped project managers focus on the ultimate goal of their projects. Formal and informal discussions and communications from various management levels had disseminated the ultimate vision throughout the organization.

But to put this vision into action requires effort, coordination, and fine tuning by programs, projects and support departments. This process is not unlike that of an orchestra. The decision on the theme song to be performed had been agreed on. The players have studied their parts. But each must still tune the instrument and practice corporately again and again for the final performance.

As of now each project and program in WV Cambodia is rehearsing individually, tuning its instrument, playing its individual tune, while group practice is still waiting to begin. And this group rehearsal is only possible under the leadership of the supreme conductor, the Holy Spirit.

NOTES

1   Mam Barnabas, verbal communication, 28.10.94.

2   For gripping testimonies of the suffering Catholic and Protestant church in Cambodia see Ponchaud and Penhold, respectively: Ponchaud, François, 1990. *The Cathedral of the Rice Paddy: 450 Years of History of the Church in Cambodia.* Le Sarment/Fayard. Penhold, Helen, 1980. *Remember Cambodia.* 2nd ed. Kent, GB: OMF Books (Overseas Missionary Fellowship).

3   Douglas Shaw, April 1991. "Preah Sre Commune, Oudong District, Kompong Speu Province, Cambodia: A Summary of Available Information." Unpublished paper.

4   Barnabas and Paulerk seem to be a Paul-team in the "Acts" of the new Cambodia, joined in nationwide ministry. Their lives are dramatic testimonies. Barnabas serves the churches through his own foundation, Encouragement Ministries. Paulerk is officially an administrator with Christian Outreach.

5

Enterprising Christians in Sulawesi, Indonesia

David Bussau

The eighteenth and nineteenth centuries are replete with accounts of missionaries who traveled to distant lands, spreading the gospel and building the church in areas and circumstances that would relegate the movie adventures of Indiana Jones to the kindergarten. Today, however, missionaries are portrayed more as villains than heroes, and the church is under attack.

There is a perception that the church has little relevance in Western society. In fact, some people rate the religious minister at the bottom of the bottom-ten professions.[1] However, the church in Southeast Asia is growing.[2] Unlike the Western church, the historical background of most Asian churches resembles that of the early church. Common elements include being a small minority, having no Christian heritage and being persecuted.[3]

The problems and relevance of the Western church need addressing. However, this paper focuses on a strategy of the use of enterprise capital that has been effective in sustaining continual growth of the church in Two-Thirds World countries. Specifically, we will see what enterprise capital has meant for the growth of the church in Bali, Indonesia.

Maranatha Trust oportunity programs

As an young Australian businessman, I disposed of my business ventures and founded the Maranatha Trust. This venture of faith created holistic ministries within the marketplace that applied commercial business principles as expressions of kingdom values.

The opportunity programs of Maranatha Trust aim to help the institutional church *indirectly* through promoting the well-being of its members—to encourage them to take Christ into their daily lives and act accordingly. This manifests itself in the many forms of expression of love for one's neighbors, whoever they may be. It inculcates elements of honor, integrity, trust, respect and dignity. This has resulted in increases in offerings, membership, conversions and community cooperative spirit. To an extent, these increases have resulted from activities of partner agencies that bring people into contact with the church.

Discussions with pastors and local partner agencies often give glimpses of the Holy Spirit working through the Maranatha Trust opportunity network. Some examples:

- A partner agency in Bangalore, India, reports that beneficiaries living on one street gathered together on their own initiative to finance renovations to the local church.

- A partner agency in Nagpur, India, has begun a monitoring procedure that analyzes the impact of enterprise capital in alleviating poverty in terms of its effect on the church. They report a measurable increase both in offerings and in participation in church activities. The partner agency gives a letter of introduction to pastors to ease access to both Christian and non-Christian beneficiaries. Prayer cells have formed in slum areas that have attracted curious onlookers.

- In Zimbabwe, one woman beneficiary was so grateful for her improved economic circumstances that she challenged the elders of her church to contribute more than she was giving. The purpose was to release the pastor to attend only to church matters instead of undertaking other work to support himself.

- Another partner agency in the Philippines has pre-sented loans as money that had been blessed. Benefi-ciaries were urged to see the money lent to them in a different light.

- In Jamaica, it is said that while they have more churches than pubs, the vitality of the Christian mes-sage has been lost and Christ's words no longer have any meaning. The partner agency there revitalizes the message by witnessing through an active application of the gospel in its development projects. People ask them, Why are you doing this?

Maranatha Trust and its partner agencies are mindful that problems such as poverty, social injustice and the ever-widening gap between the rich and poor frequently have their origins in the religious and social structure of the people. Nevertheless, they focus on serving the poor through the application of enterprise capital in poverty alleviation, training and consultation, rather than seeking solutions that would provoke social unrest and govern-ment opposition.

This enables partner agencies to undertake significant roles in cooperation with governments. They have gained a place in their respective societies that has opened the way to opportunities to both serve and witness. They assist and support the growing church. In many ways, the Maranatha Trust opportunity programs have suc-ceeded in attracting the marketplace to the gospel.

Empowering the individual

There is a greater need to witness in the marketplace than in the pews. This is the underlying premise for using enterprise capital as a strategy in fulfilling the Great Commission (Matthew 28:18-20). To bring the gospel to bear in the marketplace, however, it must be seen to apply to the daily lives of people; the marketplace must accept the gospel as fundamental to its existence and operation. In essence, then, the task is attracting the marketplace to the gospel.

The application of enterprise capital in the marketplace is kingdom building; its starting point is with the poor. Its concern is to open the human community to experience the kingdom of God. It recognizes and deals with the current circumstances of the poor rather than focusing on some predetermined future goals.

Most secular organizations would see pre-loan assessment and maintaining loan repayments as their main focus in carrying out an enterprise capital effort. This approach sees success as validating the use of capital, establishing a viable business enterprise and usually ensuring profitability. Governments seeking to alleviate poverty regard validity and viability as significant factors in determining what kind of assistance to provide.

For a successful church growth strategy, however, the function of the individual in relationship to the community is a higher priority than the validity and viability of an enterprise. The post-loan process of support for the individual—the consultation, motivation and support that characterize the nature of the operations of Maranatha Trust's partner agencies—achieves a higher degree of success than other methods and is an effective means of Christian witness and kingdom building. They show the openness of Christ's love by serving Christians and non-Christians through poverty-alleviation efforts.

The opportunity programs of Maranatha Trust are holistic in approach. They look further than economic viability and growth when applying enterprise capital in the marketplace. They seek to nurture the individual through an expression of the love of Christ and an active expression of his gospel. It is, then, through personal and caring relationships in the marketplace that his truth can be expressed and the individual empowered through awareness and a relationship with Christ. The programs create an opportunity to fulfill his command to love our neighbors as ourselves. Thus they help restore people to their true dignity and identity as stewards of creation and servants of others.

Empowering the individual helps realize goals specifically related to the church. The laity can become empowered to serve the community. Pastors can be released for full-time ministry. Evangelism can become contextualized and the gospel portrayed in a way that is relevant to the community. The church can move from depending on external financial support to drawing upon its own internal financial resources.

The cost of maintaining missionaries in the field is often prohibitive today.[4] Moreover, the task of obtaining visas to enter some non-Christian countries is either impossible or extremely difficult. Opportunities to take the gospel into these countries are, therefore, limited to occasional forays in Bible smuggling or surreptitious witnessing by professionals such as teachers and doctors. Most governments are, however, open to organizations that will assist them in overcoming poverty.

The use of enterprise capital in micro-enterprise development projects is often regarded, therefore, not only as investment that stimulates a country's economy, but also as investment that alleviates poverty through income generation and job creation. It also serves to support indigenous cultures and traditional family systems by creating opportunities to use locally available resources. It contributes to economic stability within communities and encourages the use of environmentally sustainable technology.

Maranatha Trust's opportunity programs are thus in harmony with host countries' national plans that include income generation and employment creation. The opportunity programs, however, constitute a missionary strategy that facilitates an active witness of the gospel in the heart of Two-Thirds World communities. This strategy builds a highway in spiritual deserts for the blessings and harvest to come. It witnesses to the kingdom of God through the respect, love and integrity it displays to all participants in its programs.

Indigenous partner agencies

Many development organizations are working in the Two-Thirds World through already established local non-governmental organizations. This method of operation has been adopted as a matter of convenience. It has established the presence and purposes of development organizations in target countries without having to meet prohibitive establishment and expatriate staffing costs. Nevertheless, systems and methodology may not necessarily be adopted by its representative nongovernment organization, thus producing an incomplete application of its policies and strategies.

Maranatha Trust has approached its mission in a unique manner: it has created indigenous partner agencies within the host countries. Creating a new agency is easier than changing the operating environment of an existing one.

As a first step, a governing body is established, made up of successful local businesspeople who share a common commitment to the Christian faith. Care is taken to ensure the cross-denominational character of the governing body, thus indirectly facilitating Christian harmony and unity. The governing body is not the church, nor does it represent the church. It exists to strengthen the church by serving the community through its programs. Its concern is to open the human community to experience the kingdom of God.

The formation of the governing body may take considerable time. But through the development of a strong relationship between the governing body and Maranatha Trust, a process is established by which partner agency operations become board-driven rather than staff-driven by a single manager. Responsibility for the development of the partner agency in its poverty-alleviation efforts thus lies with a group of decision-makers.

The governing body hires an executive director and support personnel who, in cooperation with community leaders, identify poverty-alleviating micro-enterprise projects that need of enterprise capital. Once funds have been released, loans are made available to groups or individuals at market interest rates.[5] The partner agency implements the program, providing training, ongoing consultation and support to ensure the success of each microenterprise business. Care is taken regarding the stewardship of funds and accountability of their use. To this end, quarterly reports are forwarded to Maranatha Trust by the partner agency, providing detail of the use of financial resources, the projects financed, and the results in terms of income generation and job creation.

One key feature of Maranatha Trust opportunity programs is offering value formation seminars. These seminars give beneficiaries a foundation from which they can relate to each other, to the environment in which they live and to the community they serve. Issues such as ethics, integrity, working environment, safety and concern for employees are covered to motivate beneficiaries to view themselves and their responsibilities to others in a new light. Some partner agencies arrange classes in adult literacy and also attend to community health concerns.

The need

Asia has the largest number of impoverished people in the world. Both evangelism and social concern are imperative in Asia because of the great number of unevangelized peoples and gross social injustice.[6] Also, Christians have historically built their social responsibility upon the foundation of evangelism. To quote Rene Padilla:

> There is no place for evangelism that, as it goes by the man who was assaulted by thieves on the road from Jerusalem to Jericho, sees in him only a soul that must be saved and ignores the man.[7]

Given that social concern can be a bridge to evangelism, we need to examine our role and effectiveness in relation to the growing church and, where necessary, develop our strategies accordingly. As Dr. Michael Green points out:

> It is a matter of root and fruit. The only gospel worth having is rooted in an encounter with the living God which has, as its necessary fruit and stamp of authenticity, a passionate concern for people's needs.[8]

The question, then, to be examined in this chapter is, How effective are our activities in supporting a growing church? This paper will look at the use of enterprise capital by an indigenous partner agency in the village of Sumbersari, Central Sulawesi, Indonesia. This example has been selected because the origins of the partner agency can be shown to relate directly to the expressed needs of the local church.

The opportunity network

The formation of partner agencies represents a strategy of evangelism that has, as its foundation, a church-initiated policy of development to alleviate poverty. This was conceived by the Christian Protestant Church of Bali in conjunction with Maranatha Trust and its development organization *Maha Bhoga Marga*. Perhaps the words of Dr. Bruce Nicholls, a veteran missionary, best express the thinking of the church:

> If we turn a blind eye to the suffering, to the social oppression, the alienation and loneliness of people, let us not be surprised if people turn a deaf ear to our message of eternal salvation.[9]

This strategy of evangelism led to the formation of partner agencies within the Maranatha Trust opportunity network. The strategy was a response to perceptions of the spiritual, social and physical needs of the people of Bali—an island that for centuries had been saturated in Balinese-Hinduism, a religion of fear.

Two main problems faced the Christian Protestant Church in Bali in the early seventies: how to make the church relevant to the Balinese community and how to free it from the influences of its colonial past. In 1972 the Synod of the Christian Protestant Church in Bali met at Abianbase under the leadership of Bishop Wayan Mastra. It developed policies of action that would greatly determine its future.

These policies focused on witness, fellowship and service. In the latter area, recognition was given to the needs of the poor. (Even today, some 22 percent live below the official poverty line.) Those living in poverty had become resigned to an attitude of helplessness and hopelessness in circumstances that they regarded as unchangeable—an attitude instilled by centuries of Dutch colonialism and reinforced by the Balinese-Hindu caste system.

The synod was very much aware of the circumstances of the poor in Bali and, while it sought to be a force in the alleviation of poverty, it was hamstrung by its own lack of financial resources.[10] It felt an urgent need to transform the church from a begging position to a blessing position. It also needed to find a way of changing people's traditional thinking. By 1975 the church had set up a small economic development effort, but it was neither community-oriented nor successful. The church realized that it lacked the necessary expertise for successful economic development efforts.

The solution to this situation came in a most unusual way. In 1976 a horrific earthquake destroyed much of the village of Blimbingsari, including the church building. The effects of the earthquake brought the Christian Protestant Church in Bali into partnership with the Maranatha Trust, which became involved in the rehabilitation of the village, including the construction of the new church building.

The new partnership would benefit the poor in many countries for years to come. Participation in constructing a church building at Blimbingsari drew Maranatha Trust into many related community projects that created jobs and improved the economic circumstances of those affected. In response to a growing awareness of the need for a means of effectively financing projects, Maranatha Trust created a revolving credit system to facilitate the development efforts of the church.

This opened the way for establishing the development arm of the church. *Maha Bhoga Marga* (MBM) was born in anticipation that stimulation of the economic development of the community would increase income levels of individual church members. This would, in turn, increase tithing and move the church away from reliance on Western financial support. (In translation, *Maha Bhoga Marga* is rendered as "the path to sufficient food," but the literal translation is "the most excellent way to both physical and spiritual food, based on a right relationship with God and others").[11]

A visitor to MBM today will see an operation that is actively pursuing the alleviation of poverty as determined by the synod in that historic meeting in 1972. MBM sees its work as paralleling that of the parable of the loaves and fishes. Jesus asked his disciples to form the people into groups and then, after giving thanks over the loaves and the fish, he fed the five thousand. A great bulk of the activity of MBM focuses on creating small groups of people and supplying them with the means to create both jobs and income and thus feed themselves and their families.

The Indonesian Government has implemented a number of poverty alleviation programs. Those who have been recipients of assistance from both the government and MBM report a marked difference. "The government came, gave us pigs and went on their way. MBM also came, but they stayed and supported us with ongoing consultation, care and help."[12] This highlights the difference between man's concept of self-sufficiency and the relevance of God. It also underlines Reinhold Niebuhr's view that the ethical system of the secular framework prevents it from bringing effective social reforms because it substitutes man's efforts and situational ethics for God's ethical absolutes.[13]

The effectiveness of MBM's work in the community is noteworthy. One group of beneficiaries at Ambiyansari has won an award from the government for their productivity in animal husbandry. They feel confident that they will achieve national recognition and that this will present them with an excellent opportunity to witness to their Hindu brothers and sisters. They claimed that already Hindus were walking alongside Christians as they witnessed examples of Christian love, freedom and economic well-being. Pastors of the Christian Protestant Church in Bali attribute an increase in offerings to the work of MBM in helping their parishioners improve their economic circumstances.

Some 80 percent of the people served by MBM are Balinese-Hindus. They are not ignorant of the source of the assistance they are receiving. They know it comes from a Christian foundation. They know that it comes as an expression of Christ's commandment to love one another. In fact, so taken are they by the manner in which the staff of MBM operate, they will demand that training, commence with worship should anyone forget. They will also attend church with Christians and even join them in making offerings at Christian harvest festivals (although this might be seen as "hedging bets").

If Balinese-Hindus, who are beneficiaries of MBM's programs, become so attracted to Christianity, why don't they convert? The answer has its foundation in the traumas of the past. The reaction of the Balinese-Hindu community has been such that conversion is fraught with difficulty. In a sense it is a bit like changing to Christianity from Judaism—one becomes a Christian but remains a Jew.

To the Balinese community, however, the act of changing one's faith is an act of hypocrisy; rejection is an inevitable consequence. This situation has been made even more difficult through the Balinese *adat* law or customary law, which in 1987-88 formalized traditional Balinese-Hinduism into the village culture. This law basically states that the land belongs to the village. If someone converts to Christianity, they are no longer part of the community. Therefore, they lose their land, all rights to inheritance, their right to live in the village and their right to be buried there. For the convert, there are two choices: retract or leave.

Transmigration

The Christian Protestant Church in Bali saw an answer to this unfortunate situation in the generous conditions offered by the Indonesian Government that, through its transmigration program, facilitated the movement of many migrants at relatively low cost. By using its haven at Blimbingsari, the church could help Christians transmigrate to a new life. (One factor influencing this strategy was the realization by the church that with increasing generations and the resultant overpopulation and unemployment, the division of the land into ever-decreasing plot sizes would result in a diminution of the economic viability of Christians).

Many seized the initiative and transmigrated; today there are now more Balinese Christians living outside Bali than in it.

Some 15,000-20,000 Balinese Christians have transmigrated to places such as Kalimantan, Timor, Irian Jaya, Sumatra, Sumbawa and Sulawesi.

The Christian Protestant Church in Bali sent four missionaries to work in Sulawesi. MBM, as the church's development arm, gave intended transmigrants relevant knowledge and skills to help them assimilate into the new life ahead of them. Projects subsequently selected needed to focus on the spiritual and social development of transmigrants. Among the criteria listed for project selection was the following:

> Projects should be structured in such a way that they reflect and promote an *active witness to the Lordship of Christ*, his concern for the poor, and the demands of this Lordship for repentance, faith and a lifestyle of obedience and service.[14]

The introduction of "green revolution" rice into Central Sulawesi in 1965 had a significant effect on transmigration. The rapid growth of hybrid varieties of rice led to a shortage of labor and a call for more families to transmigrate to the area. In 1967

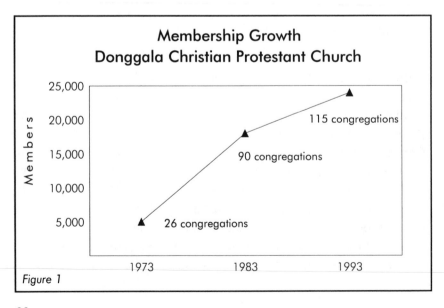

Figure 1

200 families transmigrated to the area. All had connections with previous migrants. In succeeding years further transmigration to Parigi took place (almost three quarters of them were Christians): in 1970, 300 families, in 1971, 500, in 1972, 1,500 families. Despite a government decision to halt recruitment and reserve the remaining land for normal population growth, 2,000 more people transmigrated in 1973. They were welcomed by the locals; this was testimony in itself to the labor shortages felt at the time. The World Bank, in a January 1979 report, described this movement of Balinese to Central Sulawesi as "spontaneous, Balinese and unusually successful."[15]

In Central Sulawesi there are four synods, the first of which started in 1965. The Donggala Synod had 115 congregations with 24,000 members as of 1993. (Figure 1 shows the significant church growth from 1973 to 1993.) The population of Donggala is 25 percent Christian, 35 percent Hindu and 40 percent Muslim. Before 1965 there were some Christians in the area who had transmigrated. The church in Donggala cooperated with the church in Bali in preparing the way for transmigrants—an effort they began in 1973.

The reasons for the growth of the church in Donggala have been transmigration, evangelism and biological growth. According to Gusti Bagus Sudiadnjana, the bishop of Donggala:

> The reason most transmigrants from Bali entered Christianity varied. There were those who genuinely wished to be saved and this was the dominant factor in just about all cases because of the fact of Eternal Salvation and the expectation that Christ would return. Some approached the church Board and asked to become Christians. Others simply started attending church. Some had agreed with the Transmigrant Group Head that they would become Christians when they arrived, because they feared the persecution meted out to Christians in Bali. A further issue was that many believed they would not get land unless they became Christians. (Indeed, one Pentecostal village elder maintained that anyone wanting to live in his village had to become a Christian.)[16]

Overall, the growth of the church has been one of steady increase. In 1993, for example, five new congregations emerged comprising 83 families. Eighty percent of these were new Christians.

A new partner agency: Titian Budi Luhur

In 1989 the partner agency Titian Budi Luhur (TBL) was established in Sumbersari, Central Sulawesi, after the Donggala Synod appealed to the church in Bali. The synod recognized the need for economic development assistance to those living in impoverished circumstances. The church in Bali, in consultation with MBM and Maranatha Trust, established the partner agency.

Today 44 percent of TBL's 386 beneficiaries are Christian, 36 percent Muslim and 20 percent Hindu. A further 1,947 farmers (whose religious affiliation is not known) participate in a rice bank. Cooperatives were formed by TBL to give greater control over prices by enabling storage of rice for lengthy periods using a special type of sacking.

Incidentally, certain Muslims tried to discredit *Titian Budi Luhur* by accusing the agency of operating in contravention of *pancasila*, a policy of the Indonesian Government that recognizes five religions and their right to exist free from interference. This charge was fully investigated by a number of government officials and found baseless.

One of TBL's objectives is to give youth of the area a focus within their own village so that even if they are forced to leave to further their education, their roots and the prospect of employment will draw them back to the village. Similar to other partner agencies throughout the Maranatha Trust opportunity network, TBL addresses the problem of urban migration by creating employment opportunities within local villages. TBL also seeks to encourage farmers to diversify and protect themselves against capricious fluctuations in the price of rice.

Assistance from the partner agency is available to all, without respect to faith, but staff take care to ensure that beneficiaries are aware of its Christian foundation. Interestingly enough, one staff member is a Hindu who regards his role as that of serving the community.

TBL, like most partner agencies of Maranatha Trust, assists the church in many ways, including finance and facilities. Pastors are trained on the premises, and youth receive training and motivation in serving the community.

The agency uses the enterprise capital it receives to finance a variety of projects. These range from loans of US$25 to major group loans of US$1,500 or more.

It is inspiring to see the reaction of the community to the work of TBL and its staff. It has a high reputation throughout the community and is widely regarded as an organization of integrity that serves to help the poor. Its Christian profile is never far from view. In training beneficiaries, for example, biblical figures such as Moses and David illustrate aspects of leadership.

Nevertheless, the agency does not hesitate to use non-Christians as training leaders. The objective is to provide the best training available.

Applying the gospel

The staff of TBL are encouraged to show friendship, love and openness to all beneficiaries. They become more than providers of finance. They show a preparedness to help the beneficiary in all problems. Often, they become counselors, sharing in fellowship with beneficiaries and seeking to encourage them to a successful completion of their project.

This support and encouragement has inspired some beneficiaries to go beyond the project into other enterprises. Farmers belonging to a rice bank cooperative, for example, have not only pursued their agricultural objectives but have also opened a community store.

The consequences of applying enterprise capital in this manner have been remarkable. In terms of the growing church, the increased income of the congregation has, according to the local pastor, resulted in an increase in weekly offerings. Further, a survey by the author in September 1993 showed that, in addition to weekly offerings, 30 percent of donations to the church could be directly traced to current beneficiaries of TBL.[17] This financial boost to the church has enabled it to expand its programs and meet the needs of poor pastors.

The activity of TBL in creating and stimulating economic activity in Sumbersari has drawn outsiders into the area in search of employment. TBL staff report with some amusement that some newcomers found not only employment within TBL projects, but also a Christian partner of the opposite sex—starting a relationship that resulted in marriage and a convert to Christianity.

The example of Christian concern, support and love by TBL's staff has also led some to convert from Hinduism to Christianity. Five families made this change in the last twelve months. Given the circumstances of a life free from the claustrophobic community pressure in Bali, conversion for Balinese-Hindus who have transmigrated is far less traumatic. Perhaps Bishop Gusti's words of 1986 still apply:

> The evidence of a fellowship of love became a significant factor and, in reality, the best testimony of all. In a sense, what happened was that non-Christians clearly saw Christianity in action—Christians working in peace and harmony with one another. It would seem that it was this that initially attracted them to become Christians and that it was only after making that decision that they came to hear of the gospel.[18]

The practice of TBL, as one of Maranatha Trust's partner agencies, in giving loans to the poor is nothing new. John Wesley was doing this in the eighteenth century. Yet the use of enterprise capital in a revolving credit scheme is an innovative and effective use of funds. Throughout the network, which now covers 33 partner agencies in 17 countries, repayment rates average 97.4 percent.[19] This compares most favorably with other nongovernment agencies, which have been reported as having collection rates as low as 50-60 percent.[20]

In all uses of enterprise capital, the question of stewardship arises. Careful oversight of the use of funds is practiced by TBL. In the case of delay or default in repayment of a loan, an immediate investigation is carried out. Reasons for nonpayment are discussed with the beneficiary and, if it appears that the debt is unlikely to be totally cleared, interest on the loan is reduced or eliminated.

Should the beneficiary still have difficulty meeting obligations, the viability of the business is assessed, consultation is given, and payments are either rescheduled or—if it is considered that the original loan was insufficient—further capital is lent to stimulate growth. Should neither of these options be applicable, then TBL helps the beneficiary work out how to repay the loan. Should this action and further counseling fail, collateral is called upon.

The occasions when this final step is reached are extremely rare. TBL seeks, through its counseling, to encourage and support the beneficiary in achieving a successful enterprise. TBL does everything in its power to ensure this.

The story of Riasa

The effects of TBL's presence in the community can be seen in the story of Riasa. Riasa is about thirty years of age. She lives in a small thatched house in the village of Sumbersari. Her house is of crude construction. Its walls of boards, unevenly nailed, give unplanned ventilation. Patches covering the thatched roof reduce only the major intrusions of monsoon rains. The floor is of bare, uneven earth. There is no electricity, no running water, no bathroom, no toilet.

Riasa is disabled. Her right arm and right leg are thin, withered and deformed from what appears to be the aftermath of polio. She has a daughter, about seven years old, and she looks after her aged mother-in-law, who lives with her. Riasa is a widow.

In a society where there is no social service, no old age or disability pension, no unemployment benefits and no health benefits, life for Riasa is harsh. Survival becomes a daily strategy—a nightmare beyond the comprehension of most Westerners.

TBL gave her a loan of US$25, which she used to buy corn and make small cakes to sell on the local market. She repaid the loan and took out a larger loan of US$50. She is now completing her third loan and plans to open a shop front at the entrance to her small thatched house.

Expanding witness opportunities

The developmental role of TBL in the community has made it necessary to establish two other areas of activity. One of these is a rural bank that controls the funds used by TBL for loans to beneficiaries.[21] Interest earned by the bank is used for loans and training costs and administrative development of TBL. Most creditors of the bank were previously small-loan recipients who have gone on to establish stable and viable businesses to qualify for much larger loans.[22]

TBL also runs the Kooperasi Unit Desa (KUD) or village cooperative, which plays a significant role in the life of the community. (KUDs were set up by the Indonesian Government to stabilize prices and break a Chinese monopoly on goods and services). After the farmers harvest and mill their rice, the KUD buys and polishes it for resale to the government and to other market outlets. It also sells fertilizer, pesticide, seeds and farming equipment to farmers and buys locally grown cloves and copra (coconut meat).

As in all areas of agriculture, rice farmers are always extremely vulnerable to price fluctuations in the market. Generally, at harvest time, there is a rush to sell produce and prices fall. Some 60 percent of farmers need money to pay off loans to money lenders. TBL has sought to help farmers to overcome this situation by introducing the rice bank so that they can store rice and sell it at reasonable prices. It is also planning to establish, in cooperation with its KUD arm, a seed propagating unit to improve the quality of rice grown. In addition, TBL has encouraged farmers to diversify. It appears that this advice has taken effect. In 1992, livestock production increased by 84 percent over the previous year.

In February 1993 TBL, in conjunction with the government electricity authority, obtained a license for its KUD to receive payments for electricity from the 1,200 users in the area. It was required to deposit US$2,500 with the authority, but it retains a percentage of receipts and 100 Rp. for every meter read. It employs a full-time electrical technician to maintain services and anticipates putting on another ten employees in the future. This has placed TBL as a Christian foundation in a position to provide a service that can be seen by the community to be both authentic and of high integrity.

The KUD also intends to establish a small wholesale supermarket to purchase goods from the nearby city of Palu and from Java for redistribution to beneficiaries for resale. Already it receives 30 tons of sugar from the government for resale to distributors.

So, TBL is a development agency with two arms, the Rural Bank and the Village Cooperative (KUD). TBL sees itself as the motivator and the stimulus to community unification, development and growth. Its staff seek to have a greater impact on the community as they open even more to the spirit of Christ in their life and work.

Given the traumatic history of Christianity in Bali, TBL has, through the expression of Christ's love in the many development projects it has undertaken, earned great respect for itself in the community. The same could be said of MBM and other partner agencies.

This model of partner-agency, church-related community development has been extremely successful. It has done much to promote acceptance of the Christian church within the community. People of other faiths have come to see the Christian partner agencies and the Christian church as organizations they can turn to in times of difficulty and need. From the church's perspective, it is a seed-sowing activity that awaits a move by the Holy Spirit to reap the harvest.

TBL has done much to foster a community spirit of cooperative support for one another. A striking example was the gathering of 60 men at 5:00 a.m. to help a neighbor move his house.

Supporting the church

TBL's work in community development is remarkable and is a clear and constant demonstration of the love of Christ at work in the community. Yet it plays an even greater role in its specific relationship with the church. TBL contributes to the synod in many ways, including financial help for the church building effort. (A two-story building is under construction; the vision is for a church on the ground floor and a high school on the upper floor.)

TBL supports the evangelistic activities of the church. It sponsors ecumenical activities in the district. It provides facilities for training of pastors and youth. In short, it participates in all church activities. Further, TBL has a vision to establish partner agencies in all synod areas of Central Sulawesi. Communities would rally to support synods in their expansion and establish a strong indigenous church in Sulawesi.

Some pastors have made the mistake of using development through enterprise capital as an inducement to non-Christians to change faith. They have forgotten the proverb, "An empty belly has no ears for words." Obviously, this rice Christian approach has backfired, and many conversions have been superficial. In other cases, the church has had a misguided understanding where assistance should be directed. Pastors, their families and their friends have sometimes benefited ahead of the poor—and, sad to say, have defaulted in repayments.

We have learned many lessons along the way, but we have not been deflected from our task. To cease activity in the face of criticism of our motives would simply result in a withdrawal of care, compassion and love.

Effective strategies developed over several years have given Maranatha Trust and its partner agencies ever-widening opportunities to take the gospel and the love of Christ to the poor and to nurture the growing church.

The 1976 earthquake that devastated the village of Blimbingsari also led to the creation of a partnership between the Protestant church in Bali and Maranatha Trust. In turn, many partner agencies were established throughout the world. As a result, people like Riasa, the Sulawesian widow impoverished and trapped in dark hopelessness, have found their place in the marketplace. They have been set free and brought into a relationship with Christ.

Abdullah Syarwani, executive secretary of the Participatory Development Forum, has written:

> Justice does not require equality of income, nor does it require that the productive be required to support the slothful. It does require, however, that all people have the means and the opportunity to produce a minimum decent livelihood for themselves and their families.[23]

That requirement for a decent livelihood is being fulfilled in the name of Christ.

NOTES

1   *Sydney Morning Herald* employment section, October 23, 1993.

2   Dr. Bong Ro, "The Perspectives of Church History from New Testament Times to 1960." In Bruce Nicholls, ed., *In Word and Deed*. Paternoster Press, 1985, p. 36.

     According to Dr. Ro, churches in the West are losing 7,600 people each day to materialism secularism or unbelief, but churches in Southeast Asia are growing by 2,200 each day.

3   Nicholls, p. 36.

4   Jim Montgomery, *Dawn 2000*. Highland Books, 1989, p. 8.

5   On p. 66 of *World Development Report 1990*, published by Oxford University Press, the World Bank notes that "the poor are willing to pay market interest rates. . . . [They] borrow routinely on the informal market, where rates are frequently very high."

6   Nicholls, p. 37.

7   *Ibid.*, p. 137.

8   *Ibid.*, p. 39.

9   *Ibid.*, p. 35.

10   In 1975, there were ten pastors; a centrally funded office provided 90 percent of their salary support. In 1991, there were 48 pastors; their congregations provided 85 percent of salaries and evangelism costs.

11   Douglas G. McKenzie, *The Mango Tree Church*. Boolarong Publications, 1988, p. 60.

12   This criticism of government strategy is further substantiated in David D. Gow and Jerry Vansant, "Beyond the Rhetoric of Rural Development Participation: How Can It Be Done?" In *World Development*, Vol. 11, No. 5, 1983, pp. 427-446.

13   Nicholls, p. 32.

14   "*Maha Bhoga Marga* (MBM) Project Selection Criteria," no date.

15   It is reported that in other parts of Indonesia, transmigration was achieved by compulsion.

16   Gusti Bagus Sudiadnjana, "When Paddy Fields Begin to Ripen." Christian Protestant Church of Bali, Synod of Donggala, Central Sulawesi, 1986.

17   The names of individual donors are registered by the church and read out at the Sunday service.

18   Sudiadnjana, pp. 51-52.

19   Richard Bond and David Hume, "A Review of the Operations of Local Partners of the Opportunity Trust/Maranatha Trust." Institute for Development Policy and Management, University of Manchester, 1992, p. 13.

20   "Organization Review Australia and Overseas—Maranatha Trust." Australian International Development Assistance Bureau/NGP Committee for Development Cooperation, 1993, p. 17.

21   The owners of the rural bank are TBL in Sumbersari, DBB in Bali and Pupardanata in Java.

22   Support for the concept of rural banks lending to the poor is seen in a paper by Dr. Mubyarto, professor of Economics, Gadjah Mada University. The paper was delivered as the keynote speech at the Indonesia-Australia Consultative Meeting on People's Economic Development Strategy, a June 1993 conference in Yogyakarta.

23   Abdullah Syarwani, "People-Centered Sustainable Development: The Role of NGOs in Indonesia." Background paper for a 1992 Geneva meeting of the Participatory Development Forum, "International Economy, Development and Environment: Searching for Policy Initiatives."

6
Living a new reality in Kandy, Sri Lanka

George S. Stephen

Looking back at the work of the Kandy City Mission from 1970-1991, I see the pattern of the holistic ministry of Jesus of Nazareth. Being somewhat acquainted with holistic ministry, I try to comprehend it in all things I see, hear and do. I find it in every bit of the life and ministry of Jesus:

- His conception in the womb of the virgin Mary.

- Joseph's original intention to put Mary away quietly because "he was a righteous man" and his subsequent subjection to God's plan.

- The three specifically recorded temptations of Jesus as he was launching into his ministry: hunger and the pinnacle of spirituality, displaying the power of Jesus' divinity for personal benefit and glorification; bowing down to the ruler and his systems of this world to reach the pinnacle of worldly power.

- The manifesto of the life and ministry (the Beatitudes) declared in the Sermon on the Mount.

- The parables of Jesus.

- How Jesus dealt with questions put to him, particularly by scheming religious leaders and materially rich people.

- The conversation of Jesus with the woman of Samaria.

103

- The discourse in connection with the woman with the alabaster bottle anointing Jesus in the house of Simon.

- The conversation with regard to paying tribute (taxes) to Caesar and to God what belonged to him.

- The cleansing of the Jerusalem temple.

In all these, just to reflect on a few, we clearly see that Jesus challenged the politics and systems of the Jewish religion and of the government of the time.

Jesus gave inner and outer healing. He satisfied the soul and body hunger. He declared in word and deed—in his life and work—a new and excellent way unto eternal salvation, leaving us to do the same.

Jesus did not take the path of least resistance. He was no passive religionist. He was always forthright in his challenges, and he never stood on the fence or compromised. He never played safe to keep himself from trouble. He went head-on to the cross.

In the fulfillment of his ministry, Jesus withdrew himself oftentimes from the disciples and from the multitudes unto communion with his Father and God. With that power, authority and vision Jesus engaged himself fully in the ministry (social, political, spiritual)—the holistic ministry—always by the enabling power of God in his intimate, constant communion with him. In every circumstance, Jesus was found to be sufficient. He was never unprepared, never too busy, never too tired or impatient.

Historical background

Rev. Karl Sundermeier from the Lutheran Church of Westphalia, Germany, came to Sri Lanka on the invitation of the late Rev. Dr. D. T. Niles, then President of the Methodist Church of Sri Lanka. Together with some concerned Christian leaders in Kandy, he pioneered the Kandy City Mission in 1971-72.

Rev. Sundermeier became the founder and general secretary of the Kandy City Mission. A board of directors was chosen from among the Christian leaders who helped him in the pioneering efforts. There were a president, vice president and treasurer with one or two others who formed the executive committee. Rev. Sundermeier was the general secretary. Then there was an elected council with an honorary membership of 15. This structure was to satisfy the legal registration requirements, as in any establishment.

Rev. Sundermeier remained the missionary and visionary he was and pressed his way to the fulfillment of the vision God had given him. Others followed him and supported him in his work. As the vision was put on the ground with regular Bible study and prayers, the necessary finances came from many unexpected sources in response to circular letters sent to friends giving news of his activities in Sri Lanka.

At the same time, he was the minister in charge of the Presbyterian Church (Scots' Kirk) Kandy, with a worship center in the heart of the Kandy City. This church was established by the Scottish Presbyterians in 1845.

The church's founders came to Sri Lanka (Ceylon) and pioneered the Ceylon Tea Plantation industry and allied trade activities; some of them served in the British armed forces then based in Ceylon. With the nationalization of the Ceylon Tea Plantation industry and trade by the Ceylon Government, when Ceylon attained independence in 1948, the British planters left Sri Lanka and Sri Lankans took over from them. The British armed forces also pulled out of Sri Lanka. The congregation of the elite Scots' Kirk, Kandy, dwindled to less than ten members, all English-speaking locals, mostly old people.

In 1971 occurred one of the worst anti-government youth insurrections in Sri Lanka, with severe unemployment and poverty problems among educated youth—especially the Sinhala-Buddhist youth. Sinhala-Buddhists form nearly 85 percent of the population of Sri Lanka.

Against this backdrop, the Lord sent Rev. Sundermeier to Kandy—the Buddhist "Jerusalem," the temple city. With the advice and help of friends, he did a survey and identified one of the poorest villages in Kandy for resettlement in a new housing scheme.

The Kandy City Mission secured a whole neglected tea estate from the current government, which had acquired it under a land reform act. The Kandy City Mission planned a new housing scheme on this land. The initial recruitment of youths to work at preparing land for the houses found some of the youth who were involved in the insurrection, now released from prison after the lifting of emergency regulations by the government, working for the Kandy City Mission. Mostly, these youth were unwelcome in their homes, community and even in their temples because of their involvement in the insurrection.

The former prisoners who came to work for the Kandy City Mission were readily accepted by Rev. Sundermeier. They were now gainfully employed and cared for, with food, clothing and shelter. They were now traveling about with this white missionary in his vehicle. In effect, they were saying to others that they were now free and gainfully employed, living with self-respect and dignity and even rubbing shoulders with this white man. This was a challenge to those who frowned on these youth.

The youth began to accompany him even to some of the houses of Christian leaders where he had started house group Bible study and prayer fellowship. They could sit with others as equals on the church pews. At first, these youth did not accompany Rev. Sundermeier to the house groups and to the church. Yet because he gave them a ground to stand on and with him, they were recognized. They regained their identity as acceptable individuals in society.

Ten years of work went into completing 172 new houses for the settlers and the necessary offices, buildings for the income-generation projects, service projects, a medical clinic, community hall, kindergarten buildings, a playground and staff accommodations. A cooperative shop and post office were established, along with private power and water supply for emergencies.

The construction of new houses was on the basis of self-help or with the help of relatives and friends. A government agent selected the settlers from the applicants from the poor village identified for re-settlement. The Kandy City Mission was given the freedom to settle ten percent of the people of their own choice. They were selected from among poor Christians and were strategically placed, scattered among the non-Christian 90 percent, mainly Buddhist settlers and a few Hindus. All the settlers in the new houses were given basic training in the skill of orchid growing. Each family received 200 seed plants imported from Singapore and developed in the laboratory and the Orchid Nursery of the Kandy City Mission. They would grow the orchids under the direction of specially overseas-trained staff of the Kandy City Mission for marketing. The settlers were to pay for their houses through the sale of orchids to the mission.

This repayment-in-kind scheme got on well for about four to five years but after that gradually failed for a variety of reasons, such as lack of constant care, poor care by unskilled persons among the families of the settlers, shortage of water and sale of plants and flowers stealthily to outsiders by some settlers for quick cash. However, some orchids are still being grown. The Kandy City Mission also set up units for batik-making, candle-making, carpentry, cheese-making, pottery, a bakery and cattle and poultry farming.

Specialized skills development was done with selected people from among the families of the settlers. Good quality batiks were made and marketed locally and in Germany. Good quality candles, cheese and whole-wheat health bread were made and marketed locally. The bread was sold to settler families at a subsidized price to improve nutrition. Milk was supplied to needy settlers and to the National Milk Board. Eggs and broilers were marketed within and outside the settlement.

The pottery section was set up especially for potting orchids and for foliage plants to sell outside. The carpentry unit turned out all the doors and window frames for the houses in the settlement and items of furniture required by the settlers and the mission offices. Outside orders were also accepted. Training was given to children of some settlers who were not self-employed.

All these activities (except the cheese unit) are now managed by the workers. Self-management was one of the mission's most important goals.

People come to know Christ

Some of the youth recruited in the initial stages who had marginal involvement in the anti-government youth insurrection and were working in the Kandy City Mission were attracted by the pattern of life of Rev. Sundermeier. They saw that everything that Rev. Sundermeier was doing in the mission came out of what he professed as his religion. He was always available to them. He was with them in their troubles. He was a true friend. They worked for him, not so much for the money he paid them as wages, but more for the love of it. They also learned to give free service to people building houses in the developing housing estate who could not afford paid laborers.

Some of the youth started bringing friends to Rev. Sundermeier, for employment and friendship. Those who were already attending the house group Bible studies and prayer fellowships began to discuss among themselves what they had been observing in the life of their employer and benefactor, a Christian minister. This contrasted sharply with the practices of their traditional religious leaders, especially when they were in trouble and needed help. They found inner strength, self-confidence, a lightening of their burdens, a newness and wholesomeness in their new-found relationship with Rev. Sundermeier.

Some wanted to get to know Rev. Sundermeier's religion. They asked to be taught the Bible in their language (Sinhala), because they were not educated in English. Rev. Sundermeier arranged for this with the help of friends who could teach in Sinhala. The youth attended these sessions after work with much enthusiasm and purpose. They were making good progress. They showed excitement and joy in their own experience in prayer and in simply trusting the Word. They asked for more frequent classes so that they could learn more things, more quickly. However, six months was made the minimum even for the brightest before they were examined for baptisms.

So began the church growth in the virtually dead Scots' Kirk, Kandy. The youth were baptized in groups of four and five, and sometimes even ten. The membership began to swell and fast outnumbered the original remnant. This led to new problems for Rev. Sundermeier from within Scots' Kirk, from other denominations and from Buddhist leaders in Kandy.

The old-guard remnant, English-speaking members of the Scots' Kirk did not want their comfortable boat rocked: making any change in the style of worship or the English traditions; contaminating the queen's English; tolerating Sinhala translations; having unkempt native Sinhalese youth occupy the same pews with them. Some of the leaders said that the converts would outnumber them and even take their leadership positions.

Rev. Sundermeier stood his ground. He stood with the proletariat. He gradually identified potential leaders from among these less fortunate ones and vigorously undertook development of leadership among them. Our present leadership is almost totally from among the converts. They are not all "saints" by certain standards. They are still sinners who do not, by their own merits, deserve to be in the church of Christ.

The Buddhist leaders also rose up against the tide of conversion. They set the Sinhala media in motion on a slander campaign, and the tide was somewhat arrested. Rev. Sundermeier became cautious with regard to those who were seeking membership of the church. He began to show less outward enthusiasm about conversions but kept pressing on through increased group Bible studies and prayer fellowship. The converts were indeed zealous in the face of opposition.

Members of the new converts' families started joining in. Partners marrying the new Christians began to join the fold. So the Kandy City Mission and Scots' Kirk became relationally inseparable though functionally separate.

Within eight years (1971-1979), there were added to the church 160 new believers. Elsewhere in Sri Lanka, the only significant church growth was biological growth. A survey by the church growth department of the Lanka Bible College verified that the growth during this period was exceptional.

It is true that many or even most of these proletariatians came due to economic reasons; because of hunger and nakedness;

because of homelessness; because of lack of educational facilities and opportunities; because of penury. They became the grateful beneficiaries of Christian charity.

A Christ group emerges

Rev. Sundermeier was lent by the Methodist Church in Sri Lanka to assume pastoral responsibility of Scot's Kirk Kandy. When people were seeking Christian baptism through the development activities alongside evangelistic activities under the auspices of the Kandy City Mission, he naturally baptized them and nurtured them in the Presbyterian church instead of the numerically larger Methodist church in Kandy. This, of course, caused some distress for the Kandy leadership of the Methodist church. This meant revival and spiritual and numerical growth in the then-declining Presbyterian church, which had around 340 members in 1994.

The house-group prayer fellowship and Bible studies that were conducted every week in the Augustawatte settlement and in the Kandy City center of the Kandy City Mission became the rallying point, with many answered prayers. The Bible became ever more relevant in the new believers' day-to-day living and working. The believers became aware through contextualized and personalized Bible studies that the Word of God is a living reality in daily human life and struggle in the whole of God's creation. They learned that every aspect of life at every stage and in all ages finds meaning and momentum in God, the Creator and sustainer of all things. They saw in God's Word that nothing happens by accident in Christ and that fatalistic negativism has no place in their lives.

These truths became clear against the background of the traditional religions' fatalistic passivity and negativism. Many new believers saw the power of prayer at work and the incarnate Word of God operating in people's lives, in nature and in all God's creation. This new power made them "rise up and walk and leap and sing." Fear had gone and freedom has replaced the doubts and fears—freedom of sons and daughters of God—and no longer slaves of heathen, ritualistic thoughts and practices.

Of course, these changes did not happen instantly or uniformly, but took place sporadically. We pastorally maintained close watch over the lives and activities of these new believers. During the formative years, we did not employ any strategic planning except prayerful, patient and careful watching over these lives, with the ministry of the Word.

I strongly believe that what appears to be a success story of a mission reflects the measure of God's grace that his servants have experienced. They have been enabled to keep their eyes fixed on Jesus and fulfill the vision of the incarnate Word of eternal salvation, in circumspection and in joyous yielding obedience to him. ("Where there is no vision the people perish, but he that keepeth the Law, happy is he" Prov. 29:18, KJV.)

Rev. Sundermeier shared his spiritual experiences with the new believers at prayer fellowships and Bible studies. He shared how the Lord supplied the needs of the mission. The people were aware that Rev. Sundermeier never started any development work with ready cash received from some benefactor. He placed his plans before the people and prayed with them, apart from his own private prayers. He often asked for the people's prayers for specific things such as finances needed to carry forward the work at hand. Often he purchased material on credit and settled the bills when the money arrived, sometimes from unexpected quarters. The people witnessed answers to such prayers. He always started development projects in faith and faithfulness to the Lord.

The author joins the mission

Rev. Sundermeier, personally and through concerned Christian friends, recruited mature Christian leaders of proven ability and Christian commitment to be directly in charge of activities such as building and completing the houses, laying the roadways, installing water and power supply lines, setting up the self-employment units, monitoring the discipline of the settlers, managing the Kandy City center and carrying out spiritual mobilization and follow-up.

I was invited to join the Kandy City Mission in 1979. I had served the semi-governmental National Paper Corporation for more than 15 years and held a key executive position.

In 1980 Rev. Sundermeier exhausted his visa to reside and work in Sri Lanka and completed his contract with the sending church in Germany. Together with the 162-strong congregation under the Presbytery of Lanka, he inducted me as his successor in the ministry of the Word and Sacrament with Scot's Kirk Kandy.

I was released from the full-time services of the Kandy City Mission but continued to serve on the advisory council. I am still involved in all aspects of the work of the Kandy City Mission, especially the spiritual guidance and growth of the people, mostly new believers who have come to Christ through the evangelical activities of the Kandy City Mission in inseparable partnership with Scots' Kirk Kandy.

Evaluating the evangelical work

Some of the initial converts took credit for bringing their friends to the church, as though they were doing a favor for Rev. Sundermeier or the church.

I have myself baptized 177 persons since 1981, some of them children of the new believers. We are cautious and not overtly enthusiastic about accepting everyone who comes with a story to join the church. We do encourage people to attend worship services and weekly Bible classes conducted for inquirers. We keep them, if they are regular in attendance, for a year or more before considering them for baptism. There are many currently awaiting baptism.

We do not, as a rule, baptize anybody so they can marry a Christian. We encourage such people to come to the church and follow classes and attend regular worship services on Sundays. If they are in a hurry to get married, we encourage them to enter into civil marriage in the government agent's secretariat, and then follow up with a service of blessing in the church on a suitable date. We then continue with weekly classes, ensuring that they still show the same enthusiasm as before marriage to be baptized. In such cases, we do the baptism after checking their keenness in church attendance and house worship so that we make sure, as far as possible, that the baptism is the outward sign of essential inner change. This matters more than anything else. Each baptized person is, as an anonymous writer put it, meant to be "taken by the giver of faith, blessed, broken and distributed, so that the work of the incarnation may go on."

Our experience has been that if we want to swell the membership of the church, as many leaders seek to do, there are more than enough who will take such membership: youth, for their own educational purposes; parents, for help given to their children for education; youth and older people, for help given to secure employment; others, for help given to build or repair their house; still others, for financial help given in sickness or similar beneficence. We do give help for all these and more, through benefactors and social service organizations, but not for baptism.

Many people joined the church in the initial stages when the leadership was over-enthusiastic and the beneficiaries overtly grateful for the financial help they received. They thought offering themselves for church membership was a sign of their gratitude and, perhaps, a foundation for continuing material gain. Such members have left our fold, and some keep going the rounds to other inviting churches.

Still others have become annual Christmas or Easter churchgoers, with no attendance at weekly worship or house groups. They have not gone back to the temple. Still they keep in touch in times of need such as sickness. We continue to uphold them in our prayers, so that the Lord will recharge them in his own good way and in his own good time. We do not give up on them.

In Sri Lanka, becoming a new believer is materially disadvantageous, especially for people who come out of Buddhism, the country's majority religion, and especially for those who have school-age children in rural areas. The children are subjected to ridicule in rural schools and in their traditionally Buddhist villages. There is no Christian education in any of the schools. Even in the cities in private Christian schools, the majority are non-Christians and Christian children are the lowest minority group. No Christian nurturing happens in school.

If Christian nurture is absent in the homes, how much of it can be had in a one-hour worship service once a week or less often? The absolute urgency, as I see in my relationships with families and youth with problems that they bottle up most of the time, is for regular family-based (house-group) Bible study and prayer fellowship—home-based worship in community settings—as was the practice in the early church.

This undertaking requires many competent people deeply committed to following Christ. Lay people, especially, can be in the field, engaging in this all-important task and fulfilling the very mission and purpose of life itself. Otherwise, God may find the church to have lost its first love, as with the church in Ephesus according to Revelation 2.

Believers in Christ are always called upon to set an example in bitter situations. Christians have to be committed constantly— unceasingly seeking God's grace to be good stewards. People need to regard Christians as "servants of Christ and as those most trusted with the secret things of God. Now it is required that those who have been given a trust must prove faithful" (1 Corinthians 4:1,2).

Sad to say, in Sri Lanka committed Christians are far and few between among the small minority of Christians. We need evangelism and revival within the church, so that there is unity among the Christians and the church in Sri Lanka. Then the nation will know increasingly the power of Christ unto salvation.

In Sri Lanka, humanitarian services are done mostly with the motivation of attaining *moksha*—the higher state in the hereafter, after one has acquired all one can in the abundance of material wealth. For this, we need the poor with us always. Even in Christian giving, the question of what motivates giving or doing is what matters most. Many preachers proclaim a Christ of rich material blessings but undermine the command of Christ Jesus, "Take up your cross and follow me." So-called holistic ministry becomes wishy-washy.

The rich man asking Jesus, "What should I do to inherit eternal life?" (Matthew 19:16, Mk. 10:17)—and going away in sorrow after Jesus answered—is so typical of the nominal church. The expanded version of the young man's question might be, "I have had everything good here. I want it so also in the hereafter. So, what should I do?"

In Matthew 26, a woman who was a sinner brought precious, expensive ointment and anointed Jesus in the house of Simon the Leper. The disciples were indignant and asked, "Why this waste?" Perhaps to some, the sacrifice on the Cross at Calvary was also a meaningless exercise and a waste.

However, unless the Lord himself ministers to my spiritual need, I cannot be right either in giving or in doing. When I am right (selfless) in my giving and in my doing in holistic ministry, emanating from the freedom of self-giving that the Lord grants, I become a totally yielded (no longer self-seeking) instrument in his hand for his use. This giving and doing is multiplied by his Spirit. God blesses what is given and what is done in him. He blesses the giver and the receiver to his glory and to his honor. The economy of this world is self-seeking. The economy of God is self-giving.

The principles of holistic ministry and the "in-Christ ministry" portrayed in the New Testament—whether it be spiritual, social or political involvement—is rare in my experience of contemporary church circles in Sri Lanka.

I will conclude by sharing two poetic expressions that have recently helped me understand holistic ministry more deeply. I received a Christmas card that reads, "You are to be taken, blessed, broken,distributed, that the work of the incarnation may go forward." A song written by a young minister in the United Reformed Church in the U.K. says,

> Freely and completely yielding,
> everything for you to use;
> We are partners by your shielding,
> with you I shall never lose.
> Covenants are made and broken, but
> forever we shall be partners,
> With love as our token,
> Partners for eternity.

7
Love, medicine and prayer in Northwest India

Scott Geisinger

W e have seen God at work through the Himalaya Social Service in Nepal. He has enabled this medical ministry of Youth With A Mission to build relationships with the labor community of Shimla and to win them to Christ.

It would be heartless to reach out to the poor while ignoring their pressing needs. Yet meeting physical needs in isolation of a clear proclamation and demonstration of the reality and relevance of the gospel would prove to have at best a very temporal utility. Therefore, even from the planning stages of our project in January 1990, we made it our goal to plant the church of Jesus Christ among the poor and needy of the city of Shimla. Our means would include primary health care, children's ministry, evangelistic Bible studies, prayer for the sick and simple friendship.

In preparation for this ministry, Mr. Elisha Tan, the team leader, and Bijay Ratana, a Nepali believer and team member, attended the Youth With A Mission (YWAM) Primary Health Care School in Pune, India, in January 1990. Following this six-month training, Elisha, his wife Beppie (a nurse) and Bijay went for a short scouting trip to Shimla.

Shimla, the capital of Himachal Pradesh in the far north of India is in the foothills of the Himalayas at an altitude of 2200 meters. Shima is a tourist town and a state capital. It attracts both the upper class of society and those not so fortunate. More significantly, Shimla is continually experiencing an influx of population and many building projects.

Beginnings

The team consisted of five members: Elisha, Beppie, Bijay, Andrea and Prasad. Only Bijay could speak any of the local languages, and he was just coming off a drug addiction. After a month of searching for a house and settling down, the team began taking their medical kits twice a week to Bal Ashram, a nearby home for underprivileged boys.

At this point, no one was certain exactly how or where to reach out, so much of the time was spent making relationships with the local Christians and looking for opportunities to minister. During these first few months, Elisha and Bijay began to see the lepers begging on the streets and the Nepalis on the road work crews. They wondered whether these people were the ones God would have them minister to.

One day in December 1990, Bijay met Chandra Singh, a Nepali construction worker, and expressed to him the desire of the team to meet the medical needs of the laborers and other people in poor communities around Shimla. Two months later, Chandra Singh visited the team, along with his wife Kanchi, who he said was pregnant. After giving them some vitamins and chatting with them, Beppie sent them on their way. Only a month and a half later, Bijay came home with the report that Kanchi was in the hospital and was very ill.

Beppie sent Bijay back to find out exactly what Kanchi's condition was and to take her some fruit. Bijay learned that Kanchi had been diagnosed as having tuberculosis and that the hospital was discharging her with no hope of recovery since one lung was no longer functioning and the other was at only one fourth capacity.

On the following day, Bijay, Beppie and the rest of the team were at the bus stand on their way out to a ministry when they saw Chandra Singh with a woman whom Beppie did not recognize. When Beppie realized that it was Kanchi, she could not believe that this was the same pregnant woman who had visited her only a month and a half before. Beppie began weeping and asked Chandra Singh to take his wife to the team's house where they could discuss how they could help. Later that day, they asked Chandra Singh and Kanchi if they would like Kanchi to stay with the team until her health stabilized. They agreed. In March 1991 Kanchi came to stay in Elisha and Beppie's house for three months while the team nursed her back to health and gently shared with her the gospel of Jesus.

At the end of that month, Elisha and Bijay established contact with the leper and Rajasthani colonies and got permission from them to begin primary health care. They also met Prakash Rai, a Nepali man in New Shimla who ran a little home restaurant and made country liquor. He was willing to allow the team to meet at his house with those who were ill from the New Shimla area. When the next batch of students from the Pune Health Care School came to Shimla on the practical phase of their training, a regular ministry could begin to lepers, Rajastanis and laborers in New Shimla.

One of these students was a Tamil-speaking Indian who had an evangelistic heart. When he found Shankar, a Tamil speaker, living in the leper colony, he began sharing the gospel with him, eventually leading him to Christ. Following this school's departure, Steve Kalai, a Tamil speaker from Malaysia, joined our team with his wife.

At this point our ministry began to become more structured. The medical team, including Elisha, Beppie and Bijay, would visit New Shimla, the leper colony, the Rajasthani colony and two children's homes. Meanwhile, Steve and a local Christian who translated would follow them house-to-house, praying for the sick and sharing the gospel. At the end of June 1991 Chandra Singh's wife Kanchi was physically well enough to go home. Steve soon began weekly Bible studies in their home. In July 1991 a second Bible study began in New Shimla in Prakash Rai's house, which was also a bar. A third was started in the leper colony in Shankar's house. Shortly after that, a kid's club began on Sundays in the local YMCA, which Chandra Singh and Kanchi's children attended.

After a month of Bible studies, Kanchi's amazing recovery, and a lot of love, prayer and concern, Chandra Singh and Kanchi confessed Jesus Christ as their Lord on August 7, 1991. Prakash Rai was also deeply impressed by the love demonstrated by the team and the truth he found in the weekly Bible studies and the medical care. He joined Chandra Singh and his wife in making the same step of faith on the same day.

The gospel spreads, the team struggles

Elisha and Beppie were blessed with a Jeep and graciously made it available to the ministry, saving many wasted hours of walking and waiting for buses. On one of their weekly visits to the New Shimla area, where they met people from the community at Prakash Rai's house, Prithvi Tamang talked to Bijay and asked him if he could visit his wife, who had malaria. Later Prithvi would say that though he didn't exactly trust these foreigners, Prakash had said good things about them and, besides, Bijay was a Nepali, at least. Bijay prayed for Prithvi's wife, gave her some medicine and told them a little about Jesus. From then on, Bijay made a point of visiting the Tamangs' home on his weekly visits to New Shimla.

In August 1991 Kanchi delivered a healthy baby boy; shortly after, Chandra Singh and Kanchi agreed to take baptism. At this point, Elisha felt that having them baptized by an ordained pastor was important, so they asked the pastor of the local church they were attending to baptize Chandra and Kanchi. The pastor refused to baptize Kanchi, however, since the denomination had a rule about mothers waiting 40 days after the birth of a child before taking baptism. The rule bothered Elisha, however, as did the pastor's wife's talk about needing to civilize these new converts. They went ahead and had Chandra Singh baptized. However, the team began considering the need to have a separate fellowship for these new converts who were from a different background and class than those attending the local church.

On October 6, 1991, they had their first Sunday fellowship meeting. Chandra Singh and Kanchi, Shankar and his wife Laxmi, and Prakash Rai, the first five believers, were present. The service was simple, and they all shared a meal together afterwards. Later that month Chandra Singh brought Vinod and Jhalak Bahadur to the Sunday service, and a fourth Bible study began in Jhalak's house.

Steve Kalai started becoming very adamant about the need to cease all idolatry. Unfortunately, he didn't restrict this important teaching to the new believers only. He began preaching the same message to the Hindus in the leper colony, which eventually soured our relationship with the lepers. To this day, we have not seen much fruit from there, though we continue to reach out through primary health care. At the end of October, Steve left our team with a severe case of typhoid and a family who just didn't like living in Shimla. Only days later, Silas Wahab, a Hindi speaker, joined our team to take over the Bible studies and pastor the small fellowship.

Meanwhile, Elisha and Beppie began having visa problems and had to go to several different countries to get one. Also, Beppie was pregnant and decided to go home to Holland for the delivery. While they were away, Bijay and another team member were publicly engaged to be married. However, Bijay was still under probation at that point (he had just come off drugs a little more than a year before) and both team members had been instructed not to proceed with the relationship while the Tans were away. So their public engagement led to a problem. In March 1992 Bijay and his fiancée left the team. It was, to say the least, difficult to explain to the church and the community. Meanwhile, a fifth Bible study was begun in the Tamangs' home; two people from the Bible study began attending the Sunday services.

On March 18, 1992, the Tamang family, with whom Bijay had spent so much time and with whom Silas had been having Bible studies with for three months, confessed Christ as their Lord. Later they would say that the prayers and medicine that led to their father's healing from a stomach ulcer, along with the love and testimonies of Jesus' care for his children, led them to Christ.

Bijay had been carrying most of the load of the medical ministry and, besides Silas, was the only Hindi speaker on the team. Just as Bijay was leaving, the next batch of students from the YWAM

Health Care School in Pune arrived for the practical phase of their training. Three of these team members joined our team with a longer commitment, taking over the medical ministry from Bijay. Also, at about this time Ram Singh Thapa was led to Christ through the witness of his sister, the daughter-in-law of the Tamangs' and through a miraculous answer to prayer for protection.

In July 1992 Dr. George Patterson, the founder of Church Planting International and Kevin Sutter of YWAM Church Planting Coaches came to Shimla to give a three-day training session on how to help the church grow, develop a local leadership and eventually multiply. They also encouraged the team to begin baptizing the believers themselves. At this time the church consisted of about 14 adult believers, of whom nine had been brought to faith through the ministry of the team and five had been led to Christ by the new believers and the team working together. The Tamangs would later say that though they could understand none of the messages given in the Sunday services and few of the Bible studies given in their home, the love, prayer and testimonies of the team as well as the Hindi worship songs had a powerful impact on them. However, they continued to find the language barrier a tremendous hindrance since Bijay had left and Silas was the only Hindi speaker.

The team once again faced major problems when Silas, who was then pastoring the church and taking the home Bible studies, left in August 1992. The whole situation was difficult to explain to the church, but in spite of these problems, 12 of the 14 believers were baptized in 1992 following the recommendation of Dr. George Patterson. Elisha would say later that this practice became very important in the sense that it established the new fellowship as a legitimate church with authority to receive and disciple church members. Just as Silas was leaving the team, his younger brother— also a Hindi speaker—joined us for a few months, easing our ever-present language problem.

The team survived many fluctuations at this time, six team members leaving and six new ones joining. Soon, out of the original team of five, only Elisha and Beppie Tan would remain. We often wonder about the negative impact of these team problems on our ministry potential and witness to the community, especially since several members left under undesirable circumstances.

A lack of leadership

Silas' younger brother, a self-proclaimed evangelist, had suspect doctrine. Though his contribution as a translator was helpful, the team was relieved when he left for his Christmas vacation and didn't return. He was, however, instrumental in leading to faith in Jesus a widow and her sister-in-law, who Prakash Rai had introduced to the team.

Before he left, Kumari, a young female Tlegu believer from Karnataka who could speak Hindi, joined the team with the intention to do children's ministry. The dire need for discipleship and leadership in the church required that Elisha begin taking the home Bible studies and leading the Sunday services through Kumar's translation. The desire for local leadership led to the decision to send two of the church members (one young man, Ram Singh, and one young woman, Basanti Timings) to YWAM's Discipleship Training School.

Chandra Singh was slowly given greater and greater responsibilities to act as elder of the church. During this difficult and discouraging time Prakash Rai, who had come to work as a cook for the team, had a misunderstanding over a trivial matter and left the team, eventually leaving the church.

That discouraging period had one bright spot. The Christmas celebration held in the local YMCA was a brilliant success, with more than 180 adults and children present. The team was encouraged.

In early 1993 Chandra Singh became a very active witness for the Lord while continuing to work as a construction worker. In March his prayers and sharing with one family and the team's prayer for healing for their granddaughter led to that family coming to the Lord. He also brought to Christ another family, which then brought to Christ Bhim Bahadur and family, who would later be instrumental in bringing many to faith in Jesus.

Another key factor leading to growth in the church was the team's move to a house in New Shimla on April 1, 1993. Thus far the team had been living in the main town of Shimla, which meant it took one and a half hours for people in New Shimla to get a bus and ride the five kilometers and then climb a hill to get to the Sunday service each week. The move to a house in New Shimla not only meant less distance to get to the meeting but also that people from New Shimla could come anytime for emergency medical care to the in-house clinic.

Chandra Singh joined the team full time during this period, freeing him to concentrate on the ministry. Also, Ram Singh and Basanti returned from their YWAM training to join the team full time. Almost immediately, Ram Singh was given charge of the home Bible studies and the leadership of the church under the guidance of Elisha. Unfortunately, Chandra Singh left the team and the church not long after Ram Singh's return due to some family problems, feeling threatened by Ram Singh's leadership, and a misunderstanding.

Also during this time, the team started a preschool ministry to promote education among the children of the church. The medical team took on another in-house patient, which led to his conversion to Christ. This eventually became a regular practice of the team, to take on patients who were without hope to live at the Center for a while, eventually nursing them back to health and leading them to Christ.

Bhim Bahadur began bringing others to church and led to the Lord an older backslidden Nepali Christian, Dhan Singh, and another young man. This practice of bringing others to the church and thus into the care of the medical team, the love and friendship of the believers, and also praying for the sick would prove to be the key ingredients that won the majority of the church members to the Lord.

Local leadership, church planting

In October 1993 Scott and Anita Geisinger, who had joined the team in September, began applying some of the principles of church planting advocated by Dr. George Patterson. Scott is an ordained pastor. He and Anita had planted a small fellowship of Garhwali believers in Mussoorie, North India. Both speak Hindi fluently.

Scott encouraged telling stories and doing dramas in order to more effectively teach the mostly illiterate congregation and also share the gospel with the labor community. Scott began working with Ram Singh to train him in how to be a pastor and to teach him how to train up others to become church elders. Anita began training two of the local Nepali women to run the children's ministry. Church decisions began to be made through open discussions in the church service following a Bible teaching given in story form. Three church elders were appointed from among the most spiritually qualified of the heads of households. Church services began to be held three times a month in the houses of the elders and only once a month in the team's Center (which served as house, office and clinic).

These changes, along with the training and new responsibilities that Ram Singh and Anita began giving the elders and local women, led to the members of the church becoming more active in their witness for Christ. Men like Bhim Bahadur began inviting many neighbors and co-workers to the home church services, and Dhan Singh (now an elder in the church) began holding spontaneous meetings in his house and inviting all and sundry to join. These men prayed for the sick and saw many powerful miracles.

Once, Chandra Bahadur, whose wife was pregnant, took her to Dhan Singh to be prayed for. Though she was in her ninth month, the baby had not moved in almost two weeks. They had been to the local government maternity hospital where they were told that the baby was dead and would have to be aborted. Dhan Singh simply laid his hands on Chandra Bahadur's wife and prayed a simple prayer. The baby began to kick and move again. Chandra Bahadur and his family gave the glory to Jesus, believed and took baptism.

Karan Bahadur was sick with tuberculosis. Finally, in the middle of the night, his breathing stopped. His wife ran out of the house screaming that he was dead, and all the neighbors came and confirmed that Karan was indeed dead. In spite of this, Karan Bahadur's wife ran to Bhim Bahadur's house and brought him to where her husband's body lay. Bhim Bahadur laid his hands on Karan and prayed a simple prayer. Immediately, Karan began breathing and became conscious. He said he felt extremely hot and asked someone to fan him and get him some water to drink. We do not know if Karan was medically dead. Whatever happened, it was a tremendous testimony to the power of God. Karan believed in Jesus and began to lead others to Christ through his witness.

Also around this time, Bhim Bahadur introduced Scott to his neighbor, Therlok Sharma, a high-caste Bhojpuri from Bihar state who worked as a carpenter. One day Therlok brought to Scott's house his friend Kamleshwar Sharma, who was having severe abdominal pain. Scott had one of the medical team examine him and give him some medication, but the pain remained. Later an itinerant Nepali evangelist and some of the members of the church prayed for him, and he was healed. Scott followed up with him and began a Bible study for Therlok and Kamleshwar; both confessed faith in Jesus. They also introduced Scott to other high-caste Bhojpuris, for whom he prayed and saw some healings. Several others from this group believed, and they burned their idols.

Planning, growing

Ram Singh, Scott, and the church elders met to set some short-term goals to see the church multiply. They decided that each of the elders would begin training up others to lead and eventually become elders and that new house churches would be established where Nepalis were living in nearby areas. This key planning time led to house churches being started in three other locations and several more families being reached with the gospel.

Several team members attended YWAM's regional conference on frontier missions in Kathmandu, Nepal. The conference inspired Scott and Ram Singh to bring more of the Nepali language, music, and dance into the church and to encourage the church to become completely financially independent. It also led Scott to decide to focus on planting a church among the Bhojpuri people. The Nepali church in Shimla began learning more Nepali songs and incorporating Nepali dance into the worship service. This was facilitated further by Goutam and Ruth Datta, fluent Nepali speakers who joined the team. The church also began having its monthly combined service in a rented hallway separate from the Center and gave 50 percent of Ram Singh's monthly financial support.

The church continues to grow but has recently been hindered by some Communist Party workers who have been going throughout the New Shimla community spreading a bad report about the Christian religion. A Bhojpuri house church has been born. Three high-caste men were baptized in October 1994. Several others expressed interest. A house church is being envisioned for the tribal Bihari laborers in the New Shimla area, who also have demonstrated a striking openness to the gospel.

In March 1995 we hope to send a team to another part of the Shimla District about seven hours away where many construction workers are laboring on a large hydroelectric project. We have presently sent two church members to be trained for this purpose and hope to have a primary health care worker and a couple of other YWAM staff join them.

Along with the other mercy ministries that I have mentioned, we are now opening a drug rehabilitation center in a former Church of North India's church building that we are renovating. This ministry will be directed at the drug addicts in Northeast India and in India's major cities. Titus, from Germany, has also joined our team and is presently seeking to begin language study with the hope of beginning an apprenticing ministry in which people could become skilled laborers.

We also want to begin a literacy ministry, if we can find the right staff. This is a desperate need. (It was tried once before without much success because the only staff available was inappropriate to the community since she was a young woman.) Some of our team and church leadership is presently being trained in community health concepts by the students and staff of YWAM's Community Health School from Kona, Hawaii, and is attempting to implement what they learn as they go. Finally, one team member, who has taken specific training to work among children, is rejoining us with the desire to establish a children's home for the less fortunate.

Evaluation

The Nepali Fellowship baptized 95 believers as of October 1994. Six of these have transferred to other churches, six have returned home to Nepal, two have left for work in other cities and three have fallen out of fellowship. On a typical week, 75-95 people attend the house church services. Attendance at the monthly combined service ranges from 60 to 100. Special occasions can bring attendance up to more than 200. Approximately 15 high-caste Bhojpuri men have confessed Christ. Three of these are baptized, and we hope to baptize two or three more of them in the near future.

We are amazed as we examine what God has done in spite of all our failures. In four years the team has seen almost all of the goals met that it had set for the first five years. However, there have definitely been some hindrances to effective ministry that we should have overcome.

For most of the team, it would have made us far more effective if we had learned the local language before engaging in the ministry. This inability to communicate has often meant that the team was forced to rely on one or two team members who could communicate with the locals. It probably also contributed to some of the misunderstandings and miscommunications that have arisen over the last four years. Also, our evangelistic Bible studies and sermons were over the heads of the local people. It would have been helpful if we had begun earlier using more stories and dramas in our communication with the mostly illiterate population of laborers.

Also, in our desire to have Indian nationals on our team, we weren't always as discerning as we should have been. Elisha's reasoning was that since others had given him opportunities when he didn't deserve it, he should do the same. This, however, often resulted in team members who were less than a godly example to the church. Several times we had to explain to the new believers why these people acted as they did and why they left the team.

At first we really had no church-planting strategy and certainly had no program for training up local leadership. It would have been helpful if some of us had taken some training in this area, especially if we could have implemented earlier some of the teachings of Dr. George Patterson. We are still working on the translation of "train and multiply" pastoral training program materials and believe that these will be crucial in the continued on-the-job training of church leaders and in the raising up of new leaders.

We also wish that we had more workers with specialized skills such as medical, preschool, literacy and training church leaders. There are so many opportunities; there are so many people who are open to the gospel. We clearly see, as Jesus said, that "The harvest is plentiful but the laborers are few."

Recently, we have been sending out a monthly prayer letter in an effort to raise up a greater prayer backup for the ministry; we realize the desperate need for this now and wish that we had begun earlier. "Not by might, nor by power, but by my Spirit," says the Lord.

It has been a mixed blessing to have locals work in the Center, for or with the team. At times this has led to their coming to Christ or coming into a deeper relationship with the Lord, but it has also had its problems. Sometimes, over seemingly trivial misunderstandings, we have had locals explode in anger and leave both their work and the church. This has been frustrating, to say the least. We continue to ask the Lord to give us discernment in this area.

Some among the believers have not always been the best of witnesses for the Lord—borrowing money and not repaying, not fulfilling commitments—and have sometimes caused the rest of the community to be less than impressed. This is improving, however, and the leadership of the church is making a real effort to see growth in this area. The recent arrival of the Communist Party workers into the community and the bad report they have spread about Christianity has also recently contributed to a slowing of church growth.

Finally, we often wish there were more high-quality Christian books and teaching cassettes in Hindi and Nepali and that there were more in these languages. We have seen how God has used these tools in our own lives and would like to make them available for the new believers.

We are amazed at what the Lord has done. We are certain that none of the fruit that we have seen has been of our own doing. We have seen how the Lord himself has used us like tools in the hands of a skilled mason.

What is the most important factor in the significant response of the laborers of Shimla to the gospel? We work among groups of people who have left their home communities for the sake of economic survival and so, in God's providence, have come out from under the social forces which would normally inhibit their response to Christ.

Whether they are Kashmiri, Nepali, Bhojpuri, Rajasthani or tribal Bihari, these Shimla laborers demonstrate a tremendous disillusionment with their societies. They are open to make decisions to become Christ's disciples as family and household units rather than being dependent on community leaders. We have also seen a tremendous impact on these non-Christians made by miraculous answers to prayer and the compassion of Christ's disciples.

In closing, we recall the words of Jesus:

> I will build my church, and the gates of hell shall not prevail against it (Matthew 16:18b, KJV).

Amen. Continue to build it, Lord Jesus! "Thy Kingdom come!"

Part two

Reflections

8
Anthropological and missiological reflections

Paul G. Hiebert

D evelopment programs are facing a major crisis. Many have failed to deliver what they promised, and most have not produced self-sustained development. As David Korten points out, despite decades of developmental efforts, we live in "a world of dehumanizing poverty, collapsing ecological systems, and deeply stressed social structures" (1990:1).

Some argue that this failure is due to the secular world view of many nongovernment organizations. If this is so, can Christian agencies bring about more lasting beneficial changes in human communities? This book begins the discussion of the unique strengths and contributions that Christian holistic ministries have to offer. The approach is the analysis of specific cases of planned ministry to learn from them.[1] The strength of this approach is that it tests theories against multivariant realities of life to determine their value. Theory and practice are linked to each other. I will examine these cases from the perspective of a Christian anthropologist.

Each case is obviously unique, and in some sense, different from the others. This reflects the particularity of history. Nevertheless, underlying many of them we see basic similarities that reflect the systemic nature of human societies, and our common humanity. It is some of these similarities that I would like to examine.

Christian holism

Running through the cases is a discussion regarding the nature of holism. It is apparent that holism is not simply the programmatic integration of evangelism and social concern. It is not trying in some way to reach a fifty-fifty percent balance between leading people to Christ and helping them better their lives.

Our Western problem with holism is the dualism that rends our world view into two unrelated halves. We sever the natural world from the supernatural, material from spiritual realities, mind from matter, science from religion, public truth from private opinion, science from faith, and social concern from evangelism. We turn to science to solve our earthly needs and to Christianity to give us spiritual peace and eternal salvation.

Holism is not simply trying to reach a balance between the two. If our world views are divided into segments, our ministries and programs will be divided. We are like the missionary doctor who said, "During the day I heal the people's bodies, and in the evening I visit the wards to minister to their souls." Holism demands the response of a missionary doctor who made it clear to each patient by his compassion, testimony and prayer that his medical ministry was in the name and power of Christ.

Holism must begin by challenging this divided world view. We must distinguish between Creator and creation but see the latter as a whole. The biblical begins with the one creation—visible and invisible, temporal and eternal, body and soul, spiritual and material. It holds that the evils against which we fight are the consequences of sin—injustice, poverty, broken relationships, damaged personalities, diseases, ruination of the earth, death and eternal lostness and separation from God.

The biblical world view also offers a total salvation that includes salvation and fellowship with God, forgiveness and reconciliation between humans, victory over sin, deliverance from demonic oppression and from structural evils, justice, peace, health and meaningful lives. In other words, it offers *shalom*. It sees this salvation as both personal and corporate. God transforms people, and he transforms their societies and cultures.

Such a world view requires that we abandon the linear concept of mechanistic causality that shaped early modern science. In this there was no room for God's acts or human choice. Rather, we must move to a systems view of causality. Humans are physical, biological, psychological, social, cultural and spiritual beings at the same time. If any part goes wrong, symptoms of the malady are manifested throughout the system. For example, social oppression can lead to psychological illnesses and spiritual depression. Similarly, spiritual rebellion leads to broken lives and bad relationships (see figure 1).

Similarly, we need to see societies and cultures as systems made up of interacting constituent parts. Societies are made up of economic, social, political, legal and ideological subsystems; cultures of symbols, myths, rituals, beliefs, feelings, values and world views. Evil in any part affects the whole. For example, economic oppression can hinder spiritual and social growth. Change in any one of these spreads throughout the system.

A systems approach to humans has profound implications for holistic ministries. In dealing with evil, not only must we treat the symptoms that appear in the various subsystems, but we must also deal with the root cause of the evil. For example, we must help

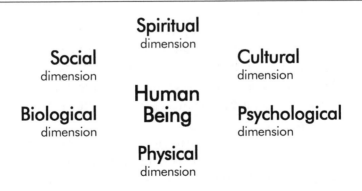

Figure 1   A systems view of human beings

the poor to improve their lives, but until we transform the social systems that give rise to poverty, we will continue to have the poor with us. We can help people to cope with psychological problems, but until they are transformed as persons through the power of Christ, these solutions are only temporary.

If we take a linear view of human needs, as Maslow does in his hierarchy of felt needs, we will first have to deal with economic needs, then psychological and social needs, and finally spiritual needs. In the end, we become so involved in the lower levels of need that we never get to their greatest need, namely the transformation of their whole beings.

The cases in this book manifest this holistic world view. Some used medicine (cases 1, 4, 7), some economic development (1, 2, 3, 5, 6), and some human rights (1) as the points of entrée into ministry. All, however, share a common vision of the total transformation of persons, and of their sociocultural systems. It is the clarity of this holistic vision that, I believe, is the basis for much of the success reported in these cases.

Culturally appropriate

A second theme underlying many of the cases is the need for culturally appropriate ministries. It is important for us to know Scripture well, for it is the foundation for our lives and mission. We must also know the people we serve so that we can communicate in ways that they understand.

We must learn the language and culture of the people we serve (1, 2, 7). This requires that we go as learners, not only when we enter a culture, but throughout our ministry. Ministry should not follow study. The two must go hand in hand. Ongoing research opens doors for ministry and makes it more effective, and ministry raises new questions to study.

We must build trust. This means we must be incarnational, living with the people and involving ourselves in their everyday lives as friends and fellow humans. As seen in these cases, we need to model multicultural and multiethnic teams that live together in harmony and mutual respect. We must include local leaders in planning, carrying out and evaluating the ministry.

These cases point out the need to make the Bible available to the people, and to teach them to study it for themselves. As Lamin Sanneh points out, nothing transforms and empowers the people more than this. It gives them dignity, and lets them know that God speaks to them directly. In communicating the gospel we need to use methods of communication appropriate to their culture. In oral communities we need to use stories, proverbs, pictures, dramas and songs, and, more recently, modern media such as oral Bibles, tape recordings, radio, movies and TV. In literate societies we should add the printed page, and now computers.

We need to recognize that God speaks to the people in ways they are familiar with. In some societies this includes dreams, visions and miraculous healings (4, 7). In other societies the people see the hand of God in social and economic uplift, and in a new sense of dignity and worth (1, 3, 5, 6). We need to build communities of Christian fellowship that create their own indigenous forms of worship and formulate their own theological responses to the problems they face based on their study of the Scriptures together.

Our mission, however, is not simply to communicate the gospel so that people understand it. The gospel calls for a transformation of people as individuals and as communities. An uncritical contextualization affirms all humans and cultures as basically good and does not challenge the evil in them. What we need is a critical contextualization (Hiebert 1984) that affirms what is good in every culture and society and calls for transformation of everything that is sinful, oppressive and destructive. It is clear in these cases that one of the attractions of the Christian message is the hope it offers of a better life and a better world as well as eternal salvation.

Organizational structures

A third theme running through the cases in this book is the need to develop new ways of organizing our ministries. Here two issues arise: first, the type of organizations we form, and second, the problem of institutionalization.

Mechanical and organic structures

For the most part, organizational structures in the West are based on mechanistic styles of organization (cf. Peter Berger et al. 1974, Ellul 1964).[2] The principles underlying such structures often run counter to essential Christian values and to effective, self-sustaining holistic ministries.[3] Table 2 shows some contrasts between mechanical organizations and organic ones.

It is clear that the success of the projects we are examining is based to a great extent on their use of organic models of organization that involve the local people, not only in benefiting from the

Mechanical Organizations	Organic Organizations
Human engineering and control	God's work and leading
Focus on institution, program and outcome	Focus on people, relationships and process
Stress uniformity	Recognize and accommodate diversity
Big is good	Appropriate size, small is good
Centralized and top-down control	Decentralized, bottom-up, empowerment of the people
Rigid, clearly defined formal structures	Flexible, often informal and ad hoc structures constantly reevaluated
Formal, mechanical roles	Negotiated relationships
Expatriate as leader, manager and trainer	Expatriate as servant leader, catalyst and facilitator
Professionalism	Mobilizing and discipling laity and new believers
External inputs required	Self-sustaining programs
Goals, work and evaluation externally-determined	Goals, work and evaluation internally negotiated
Time-driven	Harvest principle; minister until self-sustaining work is achieved
Western model of organization	Indigenous forms of organization

programs, but also in planning, resourcing, carrying out and evaluating the ministry. This assumes that people have the capacity to solve many of their own problems if they are sensitized, empowered and organized. The emphasis is on building the community (not only individuals) by seeking census through group deliberations and reflections. Through this process, people participate in their own development and take ownership over the process of decision-making and change. By contrast, holistic programs in which the outsiders distrust the abilities and choices of the people often fail, and are rarely self-sustaining (Ewert 1993).

Many of the problems in current holistic Christian ministries arise because the agencies are bridges between two organization worlds. They are organized and funded in the West and are expected by their supporters to operate as modern corporate organizations, showing measurable results commensurate to the investment. However, they operate in societies where organic forms of organization are most effective.

We must work with and modify both models of organization. We need planning, financial accountability, good organization and clear visions. We also need flexibility, loving relationships and an openness to the unexpected serendipities of God at work in the situation. We need to wed professional knowledge with lay participation. To do so we need servant leaders. The successes we see in these cases occur most often when this bridge between organizational styles has been built.

Institutionalization

A second problem related to organization in these cases is that of institutionalization. New ventures are characterized by a clear vision, team fellowship, commitment and great sacrifice. As time passes and the institution grows, formal roles, specialization, communication and accountability systems and rules of operation are needed to keep the organization functioning as a whole. In the process, those involved, particularly at the lower levels of operation, lose sight of the bigger vision, and are caught up in the tasks

139

and goals of their own departments. Commitment to ministry and sacrifice give way to institutional maintenance and job satisfaction.

There are several ways to counter this tendency to institutionalization as seen in our cases. First, effective institutions are able to maintain flexibility, good personal relationships, and a vision shared by workers at all levels of the organization. Second, institutions and individuals can be renewed through periodic gatherings in which outside input is introduced and the vision of the institution is reformulated and affirmed. This is true of a number of the projects we are analyzing.

Training leaders, not followers

A fourth thread running through these cases is the early discipling and empowering of local leaders to take responsibility for the work. Initially the expatriates must begin the work, but when new converts emerge, the expatriates' primary task becomes the discipling of these converts into positions of leadership. This does not happen naturally.

Our tendency is to train followers because it is easy and gratifying. But training followers means that the work will remain dependent on outside personnel and resources. Discipling leaders must be an intentional strategy that involves our willingness to trust budding leaders and to allow them the greatest privilege we allow ourselves, namely the right to make mistakes and learn from them. We must take pride not in our achievements, but in theirs.

The foundation for discipling is building relationships, not technical training. Its goal is not specialists, although leaders often require specialized training. Rather it is to prepare mature leaders who know the Scriptures, have a clear vision of ministry, and the people skills needed to be servant leaders. It begins with people where they are. We cannot expect to begin with mature, trained people. Discipling requires that we empower people early and respect their judgments. In the cases at hand we find that inductive Bible studies led by local workers is one of the best means of preparing them for leadership responsibilities.

For the most part, leaders are not the product of formal schooling in which the teacher sees his or her task to be the transmission of technical knowledge. Rather it occurs in the flow of life as expatriates disciple a small number of people by involving them in ministry, whether this be Bible teaching, agriculture, small loan systems and medical work. The leaders must be open and transparent with their disciples, and their teachings congruent with their actions. As seen in our cases, discipling also takes place at retreats, conferences, seminars and other special occasions where input from outside and reflection from within takes place.

Discipling is critical to team building and networking. Not only should expatriates disciple local leaders, but they should also disciple one another. In this sense the team becomes a learning and ministering community that models for the world the nature of Christian community.

Discipling does not end when we have leaders. Too often we train leaders who then train followers. It is important for them to catch the vision that their primary task is also to train leaders. This was Paul's central strategy. He nurtured some twenty-seven disciples—nine of them women—into positions of leadership, and encouraged them to train other leaders (2 Tim. 2:2). Christian leadership is caught from good models.

Establishing churches and preaching the kingdom

A fifth theme common to these cases is a clear vision of the mission of the program. This begins with ministry to humans in need, sharing with them the transforming power of Christ in their lives. But the vision goes further. It focuses on building transformed communities of believers committed to ministering to those in need around them.

In most of the cases, the workers were actively involved in ministering as members in local churches, and the local congregations were involved in the ministry of the development agency. This mutual participation is a powerful witness to the importance the workers place on the church. It is these local communities that must hear God's word and carry out God's work in their neighbor-hoods. Without a living church, the gospel is soon lost. Without the gospel, we have no church.

Several of the writers of our cases point out the need for us to go further and recognize that ultimately, mission is the mission of God. We need to recognize that it is God who is at work estab-lishing his kingdom on earth, and it is God who has called us to enter into his ministry. He is at work in the lives of the people before we enter the scene, while we are there, and after we leave.

This was the central message that Jesus preached. He referred to the coming of God's kingdom more than a hundred times. But seeing our ministry in the framework of the kingdom of God does not take us far enough. If we start with the kingdom, we can make it any utopia we wish—capitalist, Marxist or dictatorship. We must begin with the King—with Jesus Christ—for it is he who defines the kingdom.[4]

Enduring opposition

It is not enough to point out the successes of holistic ministries. These cases make it clear that effective ministry leads to persecu-tion. Neither Satan nor people opposed to Christ acting individu-ally and corporately will let the work go on unopposed (1, 4, 5, 7). Visas and permits are denied, new converts are beaten and ostra-cized, and leaders reviled. Opposition may also arise from within the existing churches as Christians fear change (6).

Painful as this persecution is, it often serves as a powerful testimony to the power of the gospel. Christians unite to bear each others' burdens, people in the church for personal gain leave, and non-Christians are forced to take note of the courage and commit-ment of these new believers. As a result, many often believe in Christ and join the new persecuted community because of the pow-erful testimony of its faith, love and new life. New believers and old learn to trust in God and his ways, and to share the Good News of God's transforming power with greater boldness.

Learning from our failures

The value of the case study approach is that we can learn from our failures as well as from our successes. In cases we test our theories against real life. When they fail us, we are forced to reevaluate and learn from them. A young businessman asked a great executive how he had come to be so successful. The executive said, "By making good decisions." "I know, but how did you learn to make good decisions?" the young man asked. "By making bad decisions," the old man replied. In ministry, too, failure can be a great teacher.

One of the enduring values of these cases is that we can read them again and again, and gain new insights into the nature of Christian ministry. As we read them, we automatically make mental applications to our own situations. We learn to examine the human dimensions of such ministry.

Prayer and dependence on God

Finally, all the cases point out the importance of prayer and dependence on God in holistic ministries. Holism is not more sophisticated methods by which we do God's work. It is rooted in the awareness that these ministries are God's work, and that with his call to service he gives strength and fruit. This is a lesson we need to constantly relearn throughout our lives.

NOTES

1   The use of cases as research data was developed by K. N. Lewellyn and E. A. Hoebel (1941. *The Cheyenne Way: Conflict and Case Law in Primitive Jurisprudence.* Norman: University of Oklahoma Press). More recently A. Strauss and B. Glaser have developed grounded theory as a formal use of cases in developing theory (1967. *The Discovery of Grounded Theory: Strategies for Qualitative Research.* Chicago: Aldine).

2.   For an analysis of the emergence in the West of the mechanistic world view on which this is based, see E. J. Dijksterhuis. 1986. *The Mechanization of the World Picture: Pythagoras to Newton.* Princeton, NJ: Princeton University Press.

3   An excellent comparison of more effective and less effective corporations is found in the working document of the Australian Broadcasting Corporation (1987) for use in transforming the company into a private sector business.

4   For an excellent discussion of the kingdom of God and the King see E. S. Jones. 1972. *The Unshakable Kingdom and the Unchanging Person.* Nashville: Abingdon Press.

REFERENCES

Berger, Peter, Brigitte Berger and Hansfried Kellner. 1974. *The Homeless Mind.* New York: Vintage Books.

Ellul, Jacques. 1964. *The Technological Society.* New York: Vintage Books.

Ewert, D. Merrill, Peter Clark, and Paul Eberts. 1993. "World view and sustainable community development." Paper presented at the annual conference of the Association of Evangelical Relief and Development Agencies, Lindale, Texas, November 1993.

Hiebert, Paul G. 1984. "Critical contextualization." *Missiology* 12:287-296.

Korten, David C. 1990. *Getting to the 21st Century.* West Hartford, CN: Kumarian Press, Inc.

Maslow, Abraham. 1970. *Motivation and Personality.* 2nd ed. N.Y.: Harper and Row.

Sanneh, Lamin. 1993. *Encountering the West.* Maryknoll, NY: Orbis Books.

9
A theological perspective

Vinay K. Samuel

This essay examines the key theological themes that emerge from the presentation and discussion of case studies in holistic ministry in Asia at the November 1994 Chiang Mai Consultation.

The case studies themselves do not present theological reflections, but some include biblical commitments and challenges to faith from the work context. Below, I identify key theological themes, describe the way they appear to be understood by those involved in the holistic ministry and attempt to provide a biblical and theological analysis of the work done at the consultation.

The understanding of holistic ministry

The case studies present a broad range of approaches to holistic ministry. Most see holistic ministry as primarily the activity of church planting while responding to physical and social needs of people. Some begin with the vision of transforming individuals and communities in all areas of life—spiritual, economical and social—and then develop a strategy that conforms to that vision.

Those whose starting point is a vision of transformation recognize the interrelatedness of all areas of life, develop ministry activities that reflect that integration and accept the gospel as also integral in its content and impact. This group begins with the understanding of the wholeness of the gospel. It is conscious of taking *the whole gospel* to communities of people. Holism is for them both the goal and the means. Holistic ministry is intentional. Such a

145

view is shaped by the biblical theme of the kingdom of God. The kingdom of God gives content to the gospel. As the kingdom of God impacts all areas of life, the gospel itself is seen as holistic in content and impact.

A number of case studies appear to see holism as a means. The goal of mission is unashamedly the planting of a church, a group of believers who have confessed their faith in Christ as Lord and Savior and come together for worship and witness. Holistic ministry is seen as often, but not always, necessary to church planting in the communities of the poor. So holistic ministry is accepted as a useful and sometimes very effective means of church planting.

The biblical and theological themes that occupy the central position in this view are evangelism and church growth. Two mandates for Christian mission are acknowledged. An evangelism mandate that fulfills the call of the gospel and has a central and unique place in mission dominates their understanding. Alongside the evangelism mandate is the cultural mandate based not so much on the gospel as on the duty of Christians to be salt and light in the world. Holistic ministry is seen as responding to both mandates in the same ministry. However, each mandate has its own integrity and they tend to run on parallel tracks.

The case studies highlight a key theological divergence among contemporary holistic ministries. A *church growth* theology of mission can expand its understanding to include holistic ministry, but the center of such an understanding of holism is proclamation of the gospel and planting of churches. A *kingdom* theology of mission, centered in the rule of Christ over all of life, seeks to impact a community with the values of the kingdom and the spiritual challenges of the kingdom. It recognizes that enabling individuals to experience Christ's Lordship is the key to holistic ministry. The different starting points of the two positions were obvious in the case studies.

The divergence between the two positions surfaces when the impact of holistic ministry is evaluated. A church growth based holistic ministry uses church planting as the key indicator of impact. The kingdom theology based holistic ministry looks at the transformation that emerges in a community that includes the planting of a church.

Clearly, two basically distinct understandings of holistic ministry are present among evangelicals involved in relief and development activities. While they may come together under the umbrella of holistic ministry, theological perspectives and orientation are different. It is here that more work needs to be done. Sharing of case studies is not adequate.

A theological dialogue based on one's use and understanding of the Bible is essential. Is the church growth approach to holistic ministry based on an adequate understanding of the *whole gospel*? Does kingdom theology of mission provide a central place to evangelism? These issues must be addressed from a biblical and theological perspective.

The role of the Holy Spirit

A significant difference from earlier studies in holistic ministry is the emergence of the role of the Holy Spirit in holistic ministry. Case studies in the seventies and eighties focussed on Christ. Christ's ministry in the gospels became the model for holistic ministry. In the past ten years, there is increasing recognition of the role of the Holy Spirit in the work of relief and development. The case studies presented at Chiang Mai reflect this emphasis.

Four key areas emerge. First. there is an assumption in most of the case studies that a ministry shaped and empowered by the Holy Spirit will be holistic. However, the evidence of the Holy Spirit's work in holistic ministry is chiefly identified with performing the *wonders* of healing, encounter with evil spirits and spiritual warfare. Exceptions are the case studies on United Mission to Nepal (chapter 1) and Issaan Development Foundation (chapter 2). Here the Spirit's work is related to cultural encounter and social transformation.

Second, some of the case studies recognize the relation between *word*—use of biblical teaching, *works*—actions to meet human need, and *wonders*—supernatural interventions of God in healings, exorcisms and other signs. The Cambodia project is a particularly graphic illustration of the presence of word, works and wonders in a relief and development project. The ministry of works continues steadily with the skills of management at the disposal of the staff. Wonders just happen as people become open to God's intervention. The freedom of the Spirit to surprise his people who are faithful in works of compassion is very evident in this case study. The intervention of the Spirit leads to a hunger for the Word. There is no particular order or regularity in the relationship between word, works and wonders.

Third, the presence of wonders appears to introduce a conflict in the Cambodia project between human responsibility and divine calling. There is a clear undervaluing of professionalism and human responsibility. They are contrasted with people-centered ministry and divine calling. An assumption appears to emerge that professionalism in relief and development ministry inhibits the free operation of the Spirit. This attitude opens the door to a new polarity in holistic ministry, namely, the alleged conflict between the freedom of the Spirit to intervene and the lack of space for that intervention due to emphasis on professionalism and human management skills.

The work of the Holy Spirit is here almost confined to wonders. That the Holy Spirit is also present in professional management activity and empowers the same is overlooked. Only the spectacular activity of the Holy Spirit is identified as definitely of the Spirit. Mundane human activities are viewed as just human and likely to be obstacles to the free expression of the Spirit. Far from strengthening a holistic view of ministry, such attitudes undermine holistic ministry.

Fourth, the recognition of the central role of the Holy Spirit in holistic ministry enables the introduction of the understanding of *spiritual warfare* into relief and development activity. Spiritual warfare is identified not only in battling the tyranny of unbelief and untruth in individual and community religious life but also in addressing aspects of people's cultures that militate against development. Spiritual warfare is seen as the key strategy for empowering individuals and communities in their struggle to overcome poverty. This understanding restores a mission dimension to relief and development work. Struggles for justice, for human rights, against oppressive forces and against poverty are also at heart battles with principalities and powers and spiritual forces.

However, using spiritual warfare as the only analytical framework for understanding the needs and problems of a community is also possible. This often leads to a demonization of the cultures of poor people. All the problems of the poor are attributed to so-called demonic aspects of their culture leading often to the demonization of their whole culture. Spiritual warfare is expected to defeat and exorcize the demonic, cleanse the culture and empower the people to develop.

While there is significant truth in such a view, it can lead to undervaluing of all socioeconomic analysis and practical actions for justice and social transformation. Such actions include restoring human rights, dismantling oppressive, unjust systems and laws, and providing access to basic services of education, health and opportunity for employment. It is, therefore, a great encouragement to see in chapters one and two a biblical integration between spiritual warfare and actions for justice.

The nature of evangelism and discipleship

Evangelistic intention is common to all the case studies. It is heartening to note that evangelical involvement in relief and development continues to keep evangelistic intention at the center of holistic ministry. The case studies contain a variety of evangelistic approaches.

The evangelistic intention of United Mission to Nepal (chapter one) is expressed in its lifestyle witness. While conforming to the spirit and letter of its agreement with the State, UMN missionaries actively involve themselves with local Christians and strengthen local witnesses through their lifestyle. Where there is freedom to evangelize openly, projects have not been hesitant to train staff to share the gospel. Regular opportunities to share are often found in small group fellowships. Value formation seminars and other training events also become occasions for sharing the gospel.

Evangelism is acknowledged as the calling of all involved in holistic ministry. This reflects an acceptance of the *every member ministry* concept. It is also recognized that in many cases some people should be set apart as evangelists who will both train the rest in evangelism and engage in active evangelism themselves.

The case studies highlight the role of sacrificial and compassionate service in evangelism. Such service is the event that enables the community to encounter the gospel in concrete form. The "events" of service lead people to look for explanations of such Christian activity. Such explanation results in the sharing of the gospel.

Evangelism becomes *event* and *explanation* in the context of relief and development. It is a biblical sequence as we note in the first few chapters of the Acts of the Apostles. The people in Jerusalem witness strange events and ask the disciples for an explanation. The preaching of the Apostles responds and explains the events by linking them to the death, resurrection and ascension of Christ.

The role of prayer is the other aspect that is significant in the case studies. The studies do not emphasize it. Clearly, the difficulties faced in addressing complex and overwhelming human needs of poor communities drives Christian workers to their knees and to recognition that prayer is the key resource for relief and development work. Prayer also opens up doors when all appear to be tightly shut.

Prayer is most often the means that empowers the Christian worker to continue in hope and sacrificial service. The most effective result of prayer is the opening of people's lives to the Lordship of Christ. Prayer is linked with seeking God's miraculous intervention, particularly in acts of healing and exorcism. Christian workers pray, God intervenes, the people are impressed and turn to Christ. That appears to be the common routine in most of the case studies.

The case studies do not present any analysis of their evangelistic activity. Themes used in presenting the gospel are not identified. For example, it is not clear if the suffering of Christ and the biblical message of the Cross is used in evangelism. In one case, the emphasis is on the abundant life offered in Jesus.

Does evangelism in relief and development contexts major on the promises of Christ for deliverance, peace, fruitfulness, blessing and abundant life? The case studies do not provide adequate data to answer the question. Again, the case studies do not provide information on what themes of the gospel message trigger a positive response, and what themes are hard to understand initially and what themes produce resistance.

The case studies and the discussions at the consultation noted the need to recognize the Great Commission of Matthew 28 as a call to make disciples of all nations, teaching them all that God has commended his people to do. This aspect of inviting people to discipleship in holistic ministry was stressed in some projects. The Philippines project gave priority to making of disciples rather than being satisfied with growth in the number of believers.

Making believers into disciples is integrally related to the way evangelism is done and the way people first come to faith in Christ. The context of poverty in which holistic ministry is done demands that only as believers become disciples and live out their Christian lives can they reflect and advance holistic ministry in their midst.

Church and community

The case studies reflect an understanding of the church as a body of local believers whose chief resources are the Bible and the Holy Spirit. There is little sense of the universal nature of the church and the historic nature of the church. Nearly all the case studies are of ministries of organizations that see themselves as parachurch. They are not seen as extensions of the ministry of a local church or a denomination but as ministries on behalf of individual Christians from local churches.

The planted local churches develop as expressions of parachurch effort. They may develop local roots but they tend to grow isolated from communities of local churches and miss the benefit of history and tradition. The ecclesiology that emerges from the case studies is the understanding of the church in essence as local. However, many parachurch organizations themselves are not locally shaped or accountable. They are national or international, drawing support from a variety of churches and individual Christians.

Parachurch organizations are themselves not rooted in a context. Their own life and organizational culture are shaped by a variety of traditions, perspectives and visions. The local churches planted by such parachurch organizations are likely to reflect contextual ambiguity unless they are intentional in the influences they allow to shape their life.

The role of the church in the community is noted in the case studies. Some projects are committed to equipping the church to witness to and promote the values of the kingdom of God in the communities of the poor. Other projects shaped by the focus on church growth see the primary role of church as evangelism in the community. The building up of a church that demonstrates the values of the kingdom is strong only in a few of the projects. Empowering the local church in evangelism is the dominant theme.

Where the emphasis is on making the local church a kingdom community, the church is encouraged to address larger community issues of justice. Where church growth is emphasized, social action in the community that might compromise or jeopardize evangelism is avoided.

How far do the planted churches commit themselves to holistic ministry? The case studies do not provide adequate information to answer this key question. Holistic ministry should result in believing and worshiping communities that themselves should be enthusiastically involved in holistic ministries.

Gospel and culture

The case studies demonstrate different approaches to culture in holistic ministry. Most ministries assume the transcultural nature of the gospel. While the particularity and uniqueness of cultures are recognized, aspects of culture that can serve the purpose of communicating the gospel effectively are identified and used. The rest of culture is seen as either neutral and more often as inimical to the gospel. It was encouraging to see in a number of case studies the recognition that Christian workers themselves were culturally conditioned even in their understanding of the gospel.

Some case studies hint at finding space for the gospel in the cultures addressed. Continuity between some aspects of culture and the gospel are discovered and used.

The case studies show the necessity of greater reflection on the issues of gospel and culture in the context of holistic mission. Holistic mission workers need to be equipped to understand cultures from a biblical perspective. Cultures in Asia are permeated by religion, usually not Christian religion. Cultures are *religio-linguistic* entities. They provide a people with a framework for understanding their reality and a means of integrating the transcendent into daily life. Releasing the gospel into such a context addresses not just individuals but also cultures of communities.

The long-term impact of the gospel in holistic ministry cannot be judged only by the planting of a small church of believers. One must also look at how the gospel affects the whole of the communities' cultures—in value system, structures and direction.

Another area of great importance is the development culture that the holistic Christian worker takes into a community. The holistic worker not only takes the gospel but also an understanding of development into the community. The development worker is shaped by a particular understanding of progress, health, modern education, family life, democracy, participation, decision making, market reality, economic principles and perspectives, and other factors. These are also shaped by a "modern culture" of economically advanced nations.

The context of holistic ministry forces the development worker to review his or her own development culture in the light of biblical perspectives and priorities. It can be a very fruitful experience.

The case studies do not share such reflections, though the discussions at the conference revealed that such reflections are common. Evangelical holistic ministry activists have a significant role to play in sharing the fruits of their reflection concerning the nature of economic life, family life, progress, wealth and markets as they minister in different cultures and are forced to consider what is biblical and what is not. Such reflections will make a necessary contribution to the so-called culture wars now going on in the advanced countries of the North and also to the issues of Christian faith and modernity, the most pressing agenda for the church worldwide.

10
Strategic issues

Tetsunao Yamamori

The case studies presented in this book describe how development projects got started, how groups of believers emerged and what issues are strategic to effective holistic ministry. The cases have various religious and cultural contexts. We see God bringing people of varied backgrounds to "faith and obedience in Christ" (Rom. 16:26). No two cases are the same, but we can discern certain similar processes through which people come to know Christ.

I see seven strategic elements that are indispensable for fruitful holistic ministry:

- Prayer
- Holistic concept of ministry
- Appropriate staffing
- Sociological insight
- Respecting lines of communication
- Training and outreach
- Finding God's bridges

Prayer

For holistic ministry to bear fruit, people must make prayer a high priority. In many contexts where the holistic approach is desired, Christian relief and development organizations and churches face cultural, religious and legal restrictions. Hostility may await them. The people or the country may be all but closed to them.

The power of unceasing prayer and the guidance of the Holy Spirit are evident throughout the case studies. For example, ethnic Nepali Christians in Darjeeling, India, on Nepal's eastern border and many Western missionaries along the southern border have been praying for years that Nepal would open up to the gospel. Prayer has been, and now is, the lifeblood of ministry in Nepal. Margot Sluka and Tri Budiardjo have done us a great service by setting down in some detail the drama of an emerging church in rural Cambodia (chapter 4). Waiting upon God was a vital part of what was to transpire. God's supernatural intervention led to broad areas of life being redeemed and renewed.

Nothing significant happens in ministry without prayer. George Stephen tells how the power of prayer in Kandy City Mission of Sri Lanka (6) made possible an ingathering of believers under difficult religious and cultural circumstances. Scott Geisinger of Northwest India wishes that the early prayer support for his ministry had been more significant (7).

Holistic concept of ministry

For holistic ministry to bear fruit, Christian relief and development organizations must commit themselves to a clearly delineated concept of holistic ministry. The concept should be part of an organization's vision statement. The staff of World Vision in rural Cambodia did not have to wonder about the rightness of what they were experiencing; they knew that holistic ministry was their organization's mandate. The United Mission to Nepal (1) has a purpose statement in its constitution that reads:

> To minister to the needs of the people of Nepal in the Name and Spirit of Christ, and to make Christ known by word and life, thereby strengthening the universal Church in its total ministry.

The staff know they are fulfilling the organization's mandate when they exhibit a caring quality in their interpersonal relationships, contribute to nation building, incarnate the Christ-life in their character and values, and share their faith and personal involvement in the emerging first-generation church.

In recent months, Food for the Hungry has officially endorsed a "vision of a community," which states:

> The community and its people are advancing towards their God-given potential by being equipped to progress beyond meeting their basic physical needs, and having a growing group of Christians—loving God and one another, manifesting the fruit of the Spirit, and reaching out to serve others.

This is what Food for the Hungry would like to see happen in the communities it serves.

Without a clear organizational mandate affirming holistic ministry, staff may flounder under pressure. The so-called tyranny of the urgent may prevent holistic ministry concerns from being addressed.

Appropriate staffing

For holistic ministry to bear fruit, utmost care must be given to staffing. This is "where the rubber meets the road." Unless enthusiastic, vibrant and dynamic witnessing staff members have frequent contact with non-Christians in the project community, no new spiritual rebirths are likely. To be sure, God can supernaturally intervene in the lives of people without an organization's witnessing staff; this was as seen in rural Cambodia. Generally, however, the people of God must be his witnesses for rebirth to take place.

David Bussau talks about the use of enterprise capital in Indonesia (5). His church-growth-based loan program requires staff committed to sharing their faith in Christ as they interact with community people who receive loans. The staff are there to counsel clients in business matters, to encourage and guide them. The staff find motivation in the hope that clients will succeed in their businesses and come to know Christ in the process. People have, in fact, come to know Christ through personal and caring relationships shown in the marketplace.

So holistic ministry practitioners must possess special qualifications. In general, ideal staff:

- Are trained in skills of development
- Are highly self-reliant—physically, emotionally and spiritually
- Are adaptable to various, often strenuous circumstances
- Have contagious faith in Christ
- Know how to lead a person to Christ
- Are trained in long-term and low-profile evangelistic skills
- Know how to form and nurture a Christ group
- Are humble and culturally sensitive
- Have the attitude of learners

Above all, staff must sense the call of God to holistic ministry. Also, the likelihood of fruitful holistic mission increases (or decreases), in general, when the percentage of trained Christians on the staff increases (or decreases).

Sociological insight

For holistic ministry to bear fruit, staff must have accurate and appropriate knowledge. They must know the sociologically discernible facts about the people and the structure of the community.

What kind of people constitute the community? Is there more than one ethnic group? Which religions do the various groups follow? What do most people do for a living? How do people in the community get along with each other? Do people marry among themselves or intermarry with other ethnic or tribal groups? What is the form of government? Who among the people of the community have responded to the gospel?

← Research Ques.

Ed Metzler of United Mission to Nepal (1) says that the country's population is 80 percent Hindu, about 15 percent Buddhist, three percent Muslim, and two percent other. He speaks of a new assertiveness among Buddhists and various ethnic groups, a phenomenon that emerged with the advent of democracy in 1990. Such a growing ethnic consciousness should be of special interest to staff working in Nepal. The stronger the people's ethnic consciousness, the greater is the need for expatriates to adjust to indigenous culture.

UMN staff have been sensitive to cultural issues. They learned the language and culture. They usually lived in community homes rather than on expatriate compounds. They intermingled socially with Nepali co-workers, friends and neighbors. They yielded to the Nepalis for formal leadership roles. They respected Nepali preferences in worship expressions, such as sitting on the floor and using Nepali music. With these considerations and other factors contributing to church growth, Metzler is able to say that a church emerged everywhere UMN had a project .

Jeff Palmer of Mindanao Baptist Rural Life Center in the Philippines (3) speaks of a vision to reach Filipino rural people for Christ through agriculture and health care. Since 1971 the Rural Life Center has grown rapidly, and its impact on the alleviation of physical suffering is well-documented. It initiates community development work through local churches. The usual point of entry into a village is the local Baptist church. This approach, according to Jeff, has led to some successes in the initial stages of village entry because of trust that had already been established; local church members know the people in their community. This is a big plus in executing effective holistic ministry.

The case studies presented here depict various people groups—their religious affiliations, socioeconomic conditions and receptive or hostile attitudes toward the gospel—and the efforts made to relieve both physical and spiritual poverty. Only by knowing the people of the community can the staff of a relief and development organization find the best strategy for reaching the community with the gospel. This holds true regardless of whether the organization works independently or through a local church.

We find three basic modes of spiritual outreach in the case studies: presence, service, and proclamation. These three modes form a typological continuum of a gradual increase in opportunity to share the gospel.

Presence

Holistic ministry practitioners model the Christian life. David Bussau's case study (5) refers to the difficulty faced by Balinese Hindus in accepting Christ. In any attempt to change their faith, Balinese Hindus will encounter community sanctions that prohibit them from owning land, receiving inheritances, living in the village or being buried there. In short, converting to the Christian faith and remaining in the village is not a practical reality. The Christian staff in such a circumstance can only practice presence evangelism (or pre-evangelism).

Service

Holistic ministry practitioners demonstrate their Christian love through development projects. Through service, Christian staff may earn the right to be heard. Numerous examples are given in the case studies of trust relationships arising out of contacts made in the process of development work.

Rev. Karl Sundermeier of the Kandy City Mission in Sri Lanka is one such example (6). People who came into relationship with him had their burdens lightened and gained self-confidence and inner strength.

Proclamation

Holistic ministry practitioners must be a part of proclaiming the gospel when opportunities arise. Having earned the right to be heard, they must verbalize the gospel. The setting for sharing the gospel may be a Bible study group, a friendship relationship, a local church partnership, a project site or an informal conversation.

Jesus says in Matthew 5:16, "Let your light shine before men, that they may see your good deeds and praise your Father in heaven." Jesus wants us to let our light shine before men and women even if we cannot always verbalize the gospel. In appropriate circumstances, we must articulate the gospel so that people seeing our good deeds will praise our Father in heaven. Words we speak may enable people to know our Father and glorify him.

Respecting lines of communication

Christian staff at a project site must respect existing lines of communication if holistic ministry is to bear fruit. Communication is generally good between two intimates, such as between relatives or friends. The gospel flows best from one member of a family to another or between two friends.

natural Bridges

Jim Gustafson of Issaan Development Foundation in Northeast Thailand (2) has seen that ministry grow from five churches in 1977 to more than 200 churches with 3,000 members in 1993. This took place in an animistic and predominantly Buddhist society. From the start of work in 1977, the ministry adopted the holistic approach. In its second year of operation, the ministry began training the new believers, and the new believers themselves took over the task of evangelism. The church expanded rapidly as people witnessed to family members and friends.

The case studies presented here provide helpful examples of friends bringing friends to Christ and family members bringing their loved ones to Christ. The strategic importance of this phenomenon is obvious. Staff working at the project site must see to it that the new converts are nurtured and trained so they can reach their friends and relatives.

Training and outreach

For holistic ministry to bear fruit, the Christian relief and development organization or church must devise systems of training and outreach. People in the project may be invited to Sunday school classes, small interest groups, Bible study fellowships and church services—spiritual beachheads, so to speak. As seen above, the care and nurture of new converts is critical for effective holistic ministry.

Some members in each of the spiritual beachheads should be appointed to make sure that new members are welcomed, cared for and made productive members of the redemptive community. New members must be given instruction and care so that they may grow in grace, increase in the knowledge of the Lord Jesus Christ, engage in his mission and become responsible members of his church.

Only in such a process can we expect to see a chain reaction take place: new converts advancing towards their God-given potential, not only by being equipped to move beyond meeting their basic physical needs, but also by being nurtured in faith and the knowledge of the Lord Jesus Christ to become responsible members of their redemptive fellowships. Such responsible members become actively involved in reaching out to serve others, both physically and spiritually. & *Emotionally*

Finding God's bridges

For holistic ministry to bear fruit, Christian staff at the project site must constantly search for God's bridges and develop strategies to reach them. The late Dr. Donald McGavran, known for his church-growth thinking, used the phrase "bridges of God." This refers to the segments of society that are responsive to the gospel.

God's bridges in a given community may be people who have endured personal tragedy or a catastrophic event. People who are at the bottom of the social ladder—the despised, the neglected, the disinherited, the marginalized—have nothing to lose. They are often among the most receptive. So are those who have been recently uprooted from tradition-bound community and social units. Examples are refugees crossing the border to another country or internally displaced migrants within their own country. God's bridges—people who have experienced dissatisfaction—can be found in most communities. We must find them and attend to them with love and care.

As mentioned above, in the process of collecting the sociologically discernible data, investigators should try to identify those people who have actually responded to the gospel. The people most likely to join a particular redemptive fellowship are those within the community who most closely approximate the group's current membership.

Some examples of God's bridges from the case studies are the Balinese Hindus transmigrating from Bali to Central Sulawesi (5), young men released from prison after an anti-government youth insurrection in Sri Lanka (6) and the Nepali construction workers in Northwest India described by Scott Geisinger (7).

The Balinese Hindus, while in Bali, were paralyzed by conditions unfavorable to accepting Christ. As they transmigrated to Central Sulawesi, they were freed from the shackles of religious opposition, tradition and unjust law. They could follow the desire of their hearts and accept Jesus Christ as their Savior and Lord.

An anti-government youth insurrection took place in Sri Lanka in 1971 due to conditions of unemployment and poverty that were especially hard on educated Sinhalese Buddhist youth. These young people were, by and large, not welcome in their homes, community and Buddhist temples after the insurrection.

Rev. Sundermeier of the Kandy City Mission recruited some of them to work in a housing project for one of the poorest villages in Kandy, Sri Lanka. He helped the youth regain their self-respect, dignity and some degree of acceptance in the community. The young people began bringing their friends to meet Rev. Sundermeier. In time, many of them and their friends accepted Christ and became the backbone of the Kandy City Mission and its holistic outreach.

Scott Geisinger's case study from Northwest India is replete with lessons and is worth careful reading. Ministry among Nepali construction workers bore fruit. The Nepalis in the area were poor migrant workers. They came to know Christ through the ministry's medical outreach, personal care, friendship, prayer and follow-up through invitations to home Bible studies.

When a particular segment of society shows receptivity, it is advisable to concentrate on reaching the entire segment. The gospel travels best among people who share commonalities and heritage. Geisinger talks about Chandra Singh and his wife Kanchi wanting to be baptized in a church as they grew in faith, only to be rebuffed by an unkind remark made by the pastor's wife that the new converts need to be "civilized." Obviously, there is a class difference between the Nepali migrant workers and the members of that local church.

This is a sad commentary on the church. While we must be indignant about social differentiation and prejudices among the people of God, we must frankly admit that such human frailties exist among God's people and work diligently toward alleviating such unjust practices. YWAM's team leader made the astute observation that a separate fellowship for the new converts might be necessary. The staff of a holistic-ministry-oriented development organization must be constantly looking for receptive people whom God has prepared for harvest.

11
Developing the
development worker

Edgar J. Elliston

Equipping effective development workers requires situational sensitivity. A training program may work well in one location, but fail dismally in another if the basic design issues are not situationally considered. The case studies in this book amply illustrate many pertinent questions in designing and fine tuning a situationally sensitive leadership development initiative.

Basic perspectives

Some basic perspectives of the key variables will help set the stage for examining these case studies. *Christian leaders*[1] can always be expected to *influence followers* in an identifiable *context*. They will exercise this influence using three primary kinds of *power*:

- Personal power that operates through interpersonal relationships with individuals who may be influenced.

- Corporate or positional power based on one's status and relationship within a social structure through which one influences through a socially legitimized way.

- Spiritual power that is based on one's personal relationship with the Living God.

In each of these sets of relationships a person is legitimately given the authority or right to influence using the respective form of power to influence. Authority in each case comes from two directions: from the *power holder* who delegates the right to influence; and from the *follower* who allocates to the *leader* the right to be influenced. All three forms of power may be brought to bear in a given development *situation*. Christian leaders may distinguish themselves from non-Christians by their conscious employment of spiritual power.

In addition to the employment of these three forms of *power* Christian leaders integrate two sets of *values* to guide or constrain the direction of their influence and the ways they employ power. These values come from both what is revealed in scripture as a normative or authoritative set of values and the values that emerge out of the local world view where they serve.

The thoughtful integration of these two sets of values forms a critical issue. If one simply works only within the local world view and values, little enduring transformation or development may be expected. Often only a temporary shifting of resources and economics occurs. On the other hand, without a serious interaction with the local world view and values, the development leader is likely to bring serious cultural dislocation that leads to dysfunctional development. If the development workers come from outside the local culture, their own culture and world view and biblical *values* may simply cause confusion or a deep-level cultural dissonance. The goal is what Hiebert describes as a critical contextualization[2] of the two .

The appropriate development of these basic perspectives of leaders influencing followers in a situation over time in a context of shared *values* becomes the subject of the training. Using some insights from the case studies presented, this chapter examines the foundational curricular issues in leadership development. Through these case studies we have seen a range of situations in which leaders have been exercising different kinds of influence constrained by both cultural and revealed values. How can we equip others to influence as well or better in the next generation? That is the subject for this chapter.

This chapter is organized to allow you to simply read through it as an essay on equipping leaders for development in situationally sensitive ways. Or, you may read through this chapter to reflect on your leadership situation. The case studies in this book presents a range of experience that cannot be fully treated in a single chapter, but that present glimpses of the range of ways to improve training for development.

Leadership development in this chapter refers to the process of *relational empowerment* following the three kinds of power and relationships noted above. Sometimes the statement, "It is not what you know, but who you know," is a cynical complaint. However, it is in a very real sense true in a positive way. While technical and cognitive competence as well as an appropriate attitude are essential, a focus on relationships provides the basis for developing a leader.

The focus of this chapter goes beyond the technician to the one who would influence others. Relationships serve as the sources of a person's influence potential. A leader's primary *power* bases come from interpersonal, organizational and spiritual relationships. The case studies repeatedly illustrate the importance of each of these sets of relationships. In these relationships the issues of commitment, integrity, credibility and spirituality consistently run through the descriptions of what is being done in these Christian developmental situations.

While not all of the case studies address every characteristic of empowering relationships, the following characteristics are commonly shared:

- Mutuality rather than selfishness
- Permanence in the relationships rather than a transient passing interest.
- Commitment born out in action not just in words
- Mutual respect rather than a manipulation of the relationship for personal or corporate advantage.
- Disclosure rather than secrecy or a "limited need-to-know" attitude.

- An allowance of time to pass to focus on relationships and the events where they occur rather than pressure for instant results.

- A development of internalized supervision rather than primary dependence on ongoing external or foreign control.

- The development of localized structures and systems rather than an imposition of a so-called international or Western structure.

The shared perspectives among these successful case studies establish conditions that facilitate the empowerment of people in all three key relationships. These perspectives include at least the following:

- A view of *power* as an expandable potential rather than a limited commodity.

- A multi generational perspective rather than a short-term gains view.

- A positive commitment in which all of the parties in the developmental process benefit.

- A perspective that character, integrity and trust are foundational to development.

- A broad perspective that goes beyond the immediate and the provincial.

Interpersonal empowerment

In the situations described above, personal power is developed through the building of strong interpersonal relationships. Many of these relationships have emerged in an inter-cultural environment with evidence of two strong attitudes: a high level of empathy and a tolerance of ambiguity. The empathy serves to allow a one to see from the other's perspective and tolerance of ambiguity allows the relationship to continue when understanding is not possible and uncertainty prevails. Neither of these attitudes threatens the foundation of integrity. While a person may make many mistakes working cross-culturally, if one's integrity is maintained throughout the mistakes can serve as building blocks for long term relations.

When seeking to equip people to be leaders across cultural barriers, the fruit of the Spirit as described by Paul the Apostle serves as the long term foundations for healthy relationships. Love, joy, peace, patience, gentleness, kindness, goodness and self-control serve to build relationships in any culture. As one allows his or her own spirituality to show through, interpersonal relationships can be expected to improve along with the potential to influence through these relationships.

The basic biblical principle that faithfulness in small things leads to expanded opportunities and responsibility is useful in this arena. As one acts responsibly in interpersonal relationships, the opportunities for expanded social influence result.

The process of empowerment then in personal *power* centers the building of durable interpersonal relationships. In these lasting relationships the foundation of trust/trustworthiness serves as protection against doubt, misunderstandings and conflict.

Organizational empowerment

Within any social system individuals are granted the right to influence others. That right to influence may be described as authority. It is both delegated from above, that is, from the power holders and allocated from below, that is, from the people who will be influenced. People in a social system or organization grant the right to others to influence them. This right is granted based on the status of the person and that person's relationship to the social system, community or organization. The extent to which the person is trusted by the community and is seen to be competent in ways valued by the community serves as a measure of his or her influence potential.

A primary function of existing leaders is to *empower* other leaders. Some Western leaders see their function with emerging leaders primarily in a training or information and skills transmission mode. They are often disappointed when people who know what to do are not able to lead in the communities where they have been "trained." While one would not want to play down the competence in the mastering information or skills, the importance of the relationship one has to the community as a community should be seen.

It is possible to facilitate or accelerate the development of a person's relationship in a community to enhance his or her influence potential. The empowering process requires several actions by existing leaders. Existing leaders may facilitate the development of a new community or organizational leader by providing an opportunity for that person to demonstrate his or her competence and trustworthiness. Following the demonstration, the existing leader may further help by providing public recognition of the emerging *leaders* without taking credit for their contributions.

This empowerment suggests that someone in the organization or community should open the way for the emerging leader and serve as a protective sponsor. This same person may provide some instruction or orientation along the way in terms of the community or organizational culture. Other orientation or training may be needed, but at least this part of empowerment is generally needed for a new leader to emerge in an organization or community. This organizational empowerment may be described as *mentoring*.

The process of empowerment in a social system can be accelerated by the following deliberate actions:

- Assign work that is important as defined by the social system.
- Provide the emerging leader with resources such as personnel, financial, facilities, equipment and time.
- Give the emerging leader authority—the right to use his or her resources and influence.
- Allow discretion. Expect success and do not interfere.
- Provide recognition from power holders. Avoid taking credit.

Certain actions are to be avoided if the process of leadership development is to remain on track. Any of the following actions may discourage an emerging leader.

- Debilitating criticism when bringing correction and discipline. Emerging leaders will need to be corrected, but discipline should be done to strengthen and encourage the person.

- Public embarrassment. The existing leaders should provide a shield of protection for the emerging leader. The situation should be so structured that the emerging leader will succeed.

- Highly risky situations for emerging leaders. The risk should be borne by the existing leader as a model for the new person.

Spiritual empowerment

A strong focus of spirituality continued to appear through these case studies. It is my conviction—and apparently the conviction of the leaders of these projects—that Christian development workers should see spiritual power as their primary power base for influencing. Again the principles noted above apply here. The source of the power is not in the person, but in God. The person who wants to use this source of power will find it accessible only as a relationship has been established over time over time. As with the other relationships, instant spiritual authority is rare. One's relationship with God develops over time. It is formed out of an extended personal acquaintance and the practice of habits that correspond to what God has revealed in his Word.

The emerging leader needs to understand God's expectations both for him or her and for the community being served. In this process these expectations are not some strange unknowable mystery, rather they are clearly revealed in God's Word. A knowledge of God's Word then is essential for the Christian development leader. Further, the emerging leader needs to have confidence in

God's willingness to care for both him or her and the community being served. As one prays for the community he or she is serving, answers to prayer will come and provide the assurance and needed confidence.

All three kinds of *power* apply to the development worker. Each is necessary for a person to develop into a Christian *leader*. The primary power base for Christian *leaders*—even in development—is a spiritual one. However, the other two must also be employed along the way. All three normally work together. When these three sets of relationships have been established and are being nurtured, one's potential for influence can be expected to rise.

Mentoring

The role of the trainer-coach-mentor-sponsor in all these relationships is to facilitate the process. Attention given to the preparing the context, sponsorship, instruction, reproof or providing discipline can be expected to bear fruit in the influence potential of the emerging leader. While some instruction may be given in a formally structured environment, values and relationships emerge through informal environments. The development of relationships can be facilitated, but as with the growth of a plant they may not be forced. The role of the mentor in this process cannot be overestimated.

An informal mentoring process has several potential advantages including: flexibility of purpose, mutual control and level of accountability by the mentor and learner, flexibility about content, timing, delivery methods and venue, low cost, high potential for personal spiritual and ministry formation. Both the emerging leader and the existing leader have a voice in the selection of the other one. The mentor may choose to work with the learner, and vice versa.

The process need not be resource intensive, but rather may be relationship intensive. It has a great advantage over formal education in its potential for individualized instruction and reflection that relate to the immediate practical needs of the emerging leader. It also has the advantage that the mentor can intercede for the emerging leader with both the superiors and followers of the emerging leader. Because of the relational basis, world view and value change may be expected. The "comprehensiveness" and "extensiveness" of the influence may be great in the life of the learner.[3] However, a single individual can effectively mentor only a limited number of people.

The mentoring process is not limited by culture, but will be highly culture-specific. Whether one works in a peasant based, kinship-based or a modern urban society, mentoring models may be used effectively in the development of leaders.

Diversity of leaders

Even with the limited number of cases studies presented in this book, wide diversity among the cases is evident. The diversity in the physical environments, political climates, economic levels, educational situations and religious settings coupled with the cultural and organizational diversity of the development organizations leaves no question about the imperative to individually design leadership development programs.

As I reflected about these situations and the repeated references to leadership development, I could see that a range of different kinds of leaders is needed. Most of these leaders need to be able to relate in an influential way to small groups with a deep level of intimacy over an extended period. Many leaders are needed to coordinate and motivate local efforts. However, a few leaders are needed to plan strategically for whole regions or nations.

These case studies reaffirm the need for a wide range of kinds of leaders. The local unpaid leader of a small intimate group who has the potential to influence each person profoundly through all of the issues of life is an essential player in development. However, the expatriate outsider whose long term commitment in strategic leadership has been demonstrated in the learning of the local language and working through the repeated and lingering jolts of culture shock is also affirmed in these papers. The strategic thinker is needed. Between these two kinds of leaders other kinds of status and roles could easily be identified. While the distribution of these leaders varies somewhat from one situation to the next, the need for local leaders is geometrically greater than for the national or international leader.

The equipping of each different kind of leader requires a significantly different equipping or empowering response. With each kind of leader the goals, content, costs, timing, venue, selection of instructors, selection of resources, delivery system and formation will all differ.

The diversity of situations and leaders needed means that a complementary diversity of equipping approaches area is also required. While the equipping or empowerment of leaders will differ widely, the design of the approaches have some common concerns.

Table 1 provides a way to evaluate the appropriateness of a leadership training program. When the values with each concern on the checklist are identified and the local situation described, the person responsible for the training design can decide a situationally appropriate training approach. This approach may range from being highly structured and long-term to one where the focus is on imitation and modeling. Purpose is the primary concern in the following list that must be addressed at the very outset. The purpose or mission guides in setting priorities for all remaining concerns. To be situationally sensitive, each of these issues should be treated locally in the light of the purpose. Each issue then interacts with all of the other issues in a dynamic way.

The case studies' authors consistently sought to design development programs that would be locally sustainable. Sensitivity to the local culture and environment runs throughout these descriptions. While little was specifically said about it, the contextual equipping and empowerment of the emerging *leaders* is critically important for the sustainability of development.

The purpose the expatriate development worker sees for himself or herself might well parallel the purposes set out for the roles of apostle, prophet, evangelist, pastor and teacher according to Ephesians 4. In this New Testament context a clear and singular purpose for these diverse roles is for *equipping*. The word that

Purpose   The broad intent that answers the *why* of the enterprise. The specific objectives or the narrowly focused desired outcomes that provide the direction for all the other variables

Content   The informational and skill parts of the training

Cost   The price that the learner, organization, supporting community, receiving community, and society in general must pay for the learning. It may include time, financial resources, people, facilities, time, or other resources.

Control   The question is, Who makes the decisions? Who participates among the key decision makers: teachers, learners, the community being served, an external agency board, government, church leaders, financial supporters or others?

Selection of learners   Who should be selected as the learners? What are their characteristics (e.g., competencies, learning styles, attitudes, cultural biases, needs, aspirations)?

Selection of teachers   Who should be selected as the teachers? How will they model what the learners are to become.

Venue   Where should the instruction take place? In a centralized location, e.g., a school or in the context of the application of the learning? Is the question of access to the learners and their learning or the convenience of the trainer in focus?

Resources   What resources should be used? Are the resources sustainable? Which resources should be used for which parts of the training?

Timing   The questions of *when* and *how long* need to be asked. When in terms of the learner's career or life cycle or convenience should the learning take place? How long should it be—a few minutes, hours days, weeks? How should it be distributed over time?

Spiritual formation   How will the learners develop their relationship with God through the process? How will the spiritual disciplines be employed to build personal discipleship and spiritual authority?

Community and team formation   How will the person be equipped and empowered to work within the community? How is the community being prepared for the acceptance and employment of this person? What is to be done to build relationships with the community, both as individuals and as a community?

Delivery system   What will be the balance among the formal, non-formal and informal modes of education be?

Administrative support   What administrative structures will be employed to deliver what is proposed?

Table 1   Curricular issues in a leadership training program

stands behind the equipping here suggests a contextual outfitting or fitting together. The word is sometimes translated as train, perfect or men as in the mending of nets. The focus of these leadership roles is not on the functions of each role, but rather on the next generation of people who would be trained, equipped or outfitted for service. That same kind of perspective needs to be the mind-set of the development worker.

Conclusion

To follow the examples in developing a broadly based durable leadership as seen in the case studies, several clear actions are indicated:

- The development of basic competencies is required. Appropriate knowledge, skills and attitudes must be demonstrable in the context as one begins to emerge as a leader.

- Interpersonal relations need to be established through which the emerging leader is empowered to influence.

- Community and organizational relationships need to be established to legitimize the emerging leader's status and role relationships for influence within the social system.

- One's relationship with God needs to be established to shape the emerging leader's life and purpose so that God's *power* can work through him or her.

- While some leaders emerge with few active mentors, an active mentor who is already in the system may greatly facilitate the emergence of another person. The mentoring process will include the preparation of the context, the care, the nurture and instruction, protection, and sponsorship of that emerging leader.

NOTES

1   Certain key leadership variables are italicized in this chapter..
      They include leader, follower, power, and values.

2   A critical contextual model takes both the Scriptures and culture
      seriously, and then asks the church to participate in the interpre-
      tation both ways. This approach avoids the twin dangers of syn-
      cretism on the one side or a legalistic suppression of cultural
      forms on the other (cf. Hiebert 1989:101-120 and Gilliland
      1989:317).

3   See Dennis Wrong, *Power—Its Forms and Sources*. He describes
      three attributes of power including: *comprehensiveness* or the scope
      of lifestyle issues one my influence, *extensiveness* or the number of
      people who may be influenced, and *intensity* or the depth to
      which one may influence about a given issue.

REFERENCES

Clinton, J. Robert and Richard W. Clinton, 1991. *The Mentor Handbook* .
Altadena, CA: Barnabas Publishers.

Gilliland, Dean S. (ed.), 1989. *The Word Among Us: Contextualizing Theology
for Mission Today.* Dallas: Word.

Elliston, Edgar J, 1992. *Home Grown Leaders.* Pasadena: William Carey
Library.

—————, 1995. "Mentoring: A Call to Excellence in Leadership for a
Lifetime," A lectureship prepared for Lincoln Christian Seminary.

Hiebert, Paul E., 1989. "Form and Meaning in the contextualization of the
Gospel," In Dean S. Gilliland, ed. *The Word Among Us: Contextualizing
Theology for Mission Today.* Dallas: Word. pp. 101-120.

Murray, Margo, 1992. *Beyond the Myths and Magic of Mentoring: How to
Facilitate an Effective Mentoring Program.* San Francisco: Jossey-Bass
Publishers.

Stanley, Paul and J. Robert Clinton, 1992. *Connecting: The Mentoring Relationships You Need to Succeed in Life.* Colorado Springs: NavPress.

12
Modernity and holistic mininstry

Bryant L. Myers

This book is about holistic ministry. Every case is held up as a useful example of holistic ministry. Obviously, we attach a lot of importance to the word "holistic." What does holistic mean? What should it mean?

One way to begin is to ask why we need the word in the first place. If the Bible contains a holistic understanding of the world, and it does, then why is this fact worth naming? The word "holistic" must be needed because there is something that is not now holistic. My purpose here is to explore how we have come to need the idea of holism and to relate this to the eight case studies in this book.

In writing this chapter, I am sensitive to the fact that the case writers were unaware of my questions when they wrote their cases. Had they known the issues I was going to raise, they surely would have added additional material to their narrative. Therefore, I may be unfair to the facts of the cases when I point to things not mentioned. Since there is no escape from this dilemma, I plead for understanding by the case writers and apologize now for any unjust observations I may make.

The great divorce

We need to begin with the way we understand and interpret the world in which we live. In a sense, our modern world view is like a pair of glasses through which we view our world. Our world view also includes many assumptions about how the world works. Our need for the idea of holism has its roots in this modern world view.

As the foundational paradigm shift of the Enlightenment worked itself out in Western culture over the last several centuries, one of its most enduring features has been the assumption that we can consider the physical and spiritual realms as separate and distinct from one another.[1] We are taught to view the world as two separate, unrelated realms. On the one hand, there is the spiritual or supernatural world where God lives and acts, along with other cosmic gods like Allah. This is the world of religion. On the other hand, there is the real world: the material world where we hear, see, feel, touch and smell. This is the world of science.

Sad to say, this is not a problem only for Western folk. This dichotomy between the spiritual and the physical is a central tenet of what some call modernity, and this modernity is rapidly becoming the dominant world culture. Modernity is deeply embedded in the modern economic system and in contemporary information technology, both of which are being extended wherever Coca Cola is sold. This same culture of dichotomies is taught in every classroom where the curriculum has been based on Western educational models. Thus all Third World professionals have imbibed this world view as an unspoken part of their professional training.

This framework of separated areas of life is also deeply embedded in the Christian church, in its theology and in the daily life of its people. On Sunday morning or during our devotional or prayer life, we operate in the spiritual realm. The rest of the week, and in our professional lives, we operate in the physical realm and, hence, unwittingly act like functional atheists. Simply being Christian does not heal our dichotomous understanding of our world.

Paul Hiebert has helped a lot when he compares the world views of modernity and animism to the world view of the Bible.[2] The modern world view is characterized by a two-tiered understanding of the world with the physical and spiritual worlds completely separated. Alternatively, the biblical world view is holistic in the sense that the physical world is never understood as being apart from the spiritual world and the rule of the God who created it. Moreover, Christ—the creator, sustainer and redeemer of the creation—is both in us and interceding for us at the right hand of God the Father.

This comparison also calls attention to the fact that the critical questions change depending on the level at which one is functioning. The gospel addresses the questions of truth, power and pragmatics with the truth of God, the power of God and the love of God.

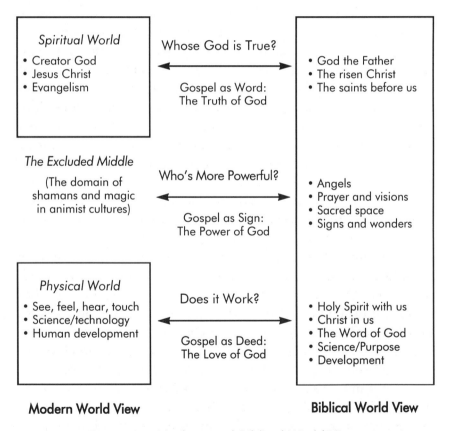

Figure 1   Modern and Biblical World Views
(adapted from Paul Hiebert)

This in turn reveals another level of the problem modernity poses to Christian mission. When we separate the spiritual from the physical, not only do we separate evangelism from development. We also separate gospel-as-word from the gospel-as-deed, and provide no home for gospel-as-sign. In the spiritual realm, the critical question is, Whose God is the true God? The answer is an idea. This frame allows the gospel message to be reduced to propositional truth, even a set of "spiritual laws." Evangelism becomes words and speaking.

At the level of the physical world, the question is, What works? The answer comes as right method and good technology. Deeds and doing are the real thing. We reduce the gospel message and evangelism to working for justice or saving God's creation.

Separating gospel-as-word, gospel-as-deed and gospel-as-sign has serious consequences. In cultures in which words have lost their meaning, as is the case in the West, deeds are necessary to verify what words mean. Saying we are Christian is ambiguous since almost everyone claims to be Christian. If we want to know what someone means when they say they are Christian, we look at their lives. The way we live and act declares to others what we mean when we say we are Christians.

In other cultures, deeds can be ambiguous. Whether we speak or not, people receive a message. Discovering water in the desert is a miracle and the technology that brings it is often interpreted by animist cultures as magic and witchcraft. Research done by MARC has discovered this repeatedly in World Vision's development work[3]. In the view of some local villagers, World Vision has outstanding witch doctors and powerful shamans on its staff. Development technology, without accompanying words that interpret its good deeds, can result in glory being given to clever or "magical" soil scientists and hydrologists, rather than to God.

We must also call attention to the inadequate way the modern world view deals with signs. Because it has no place for the appearance of the supernatural in the physical world, there is no home for signs and miracles. For most animists, the existential question has little to do with truth or pragmatics—it has to do with power. Since cause is located in the unseen or spiritual world, the critical question is, Whose god is more powerful? The fact that charismatic and Pentecostal folk have an answer for this question is a major part of the reason why they are the fastest growing expression of the church today.

The inability of the modern to deal with signs and miracles makes it very difficult for carriers of modernity, such as development practitioners, to carry out meaningful conversations with people who hold a traditional or animist world view. Development practitioners think people are sick because of germs and dirty water, while the people believe they are sick because of curses and witchcraft.

Therefore, in dealing with the gospel message, we cannot separate words, deeds and signs without truncating our message. Words are needed to clarify the meaning of deeds. Deeds verify the meaning of words. Most critically, signs announce the presence and power of One who is radically other and who is both the true source of all good deeds and the author of the only words that bring life in its fullest.

Having asserted the inseparability of word, deed and sign, however, we must not overlook the question, How do people come to faith? Romans 10 points to the unique role of gospel-as-word. Neither gospel-as-sign nor gospel-as-deed is sufficient. In other words, the gospel message points people in a direction and toward a decision. The direction is toward the kingdom of God, and the decision is whether or not to accept Jesus as Savior and Lord. So while we must recover a gospel message that is inseparably word, deed and sign, we must also understand that its purpose is to reconcile people to God and to each other through Jesus Christ.

What then should we do?

Having said all this, what concrete actions in the real world do we need to take to be authentically and fully Christian in our promotion of human transformation? How should the recovery of a holistic understanding of an integrated spiritual-physical world view change the way Christian relief and development agencies carry out their development ministries?

Holistic practitioners

We need to develop holistic practitioners. Linking a holistic understanding of ministry to practice will only take place if the people who do the work have developed an integrated world view. This is particularly difficult since all of their professional training reinforces the dichotomy we wish to overcome. We need to do several things to overcome this problem.

First, people need help in making their existing world view explicit and encouragement to help each other root out the vestiges of the modern world view and place a biblical, integrated world view in its place. This requires training that enables practitioners to become aware of the problem, and then encourages their continuing reflection on both the language and practice of their development ministry.

People who refuse to separate their professional and spiritual lives are described in the case studies of the United Mission of Nepal (1), Mindanao Baptist Rural Life Center (3) and Himalaya Social Services (7). However, from the information available it seems that the dichotomy between doing development work and the spiritual work of evangelism, discipleship and spiritual warfare is in force in most of the case studies.

Second, we must help people learn how to reflect theologically on their work. A recent study of urban work in three World Vision countries concluded: "Nowhere was there any sign of a serious or consistent attempt to enable either project workers or office staff to develop skills in theological reflection on the task in which they were engaged."[4] Bringing our work—both its results and the methods we use—to the living Word of God is critical to being open to the Spirit of God who, we are promised, will lead us into all truth. The expressions of relief and development practice that are less than Christian will only be exposed as we bring our technical knowledge and experience into an informed encounter with Scripture.

Most of the case studies point to the importance of the Bible in their work. Use of the Nepali Bible is mentioned in the United Mission to Nepal case (1). Bible studies and devotions are a critical factor in reshaping the lives of youth in the Kandy City Mission case (6). However, none of the case studies mention theological reflection. It may be that other agencies are suffering from the same blind spot as World Vision. Theological reflection is critical for the effective work of agencies, but we are reminded by the Issaan case (2) that theology is a poor substitute for the simple words of the gospel when it comes to Christian witness.

Third, we need to equip ourselves more systematically with carefully chosen anthropological skills. When our development technology is expressed in traditional cultures, there is a conflict in world views: Is healing the result of killing germs or lifting curses? To bridge the gap, we must understand how traditional cultures understand and interpret what we do; we must also clearly understand the modernity that shapes how we practice development. If we want to discover what message they are receiving, we will need the technical skills to do so.

In several of our cases, serious attention is given to developing and using these kinds of skills. For example, the Issaan Development Foundation (2) describes its task as "enabling Jesus Christ to be born into the Northeast Thai culture," using an approach Paul Hiebert calls *critical contextualization*.[5] This, however, appears to focus solely on the delivery of the Christian message. Erik Cohen's work on folk religions in Thailand[6] makes me wonder how the local people in fact interpret and give meaning to the development change taking place around them.

Finally, we need to develop a process of spiritual formation that creates what the Bible calls "eyes to see and ears to hear." If being in Christ makes us new people and if our minds are indeed being transformed, then this change should extend itself into the ways we think about and respond to the poor and do development. We need to develop an understanding of spiritual formation that gives it the same standing as we now give to our professional training of development facilitators, agriculturalists and promoters of primary health care. Most of our case studies allude to the importance of personal discipleship and holiness in some form. The Oudong Rural Health Project (4) and Himalaya Social Service (7) point to the importance of prayer as a development tool. None, however, describe spiritual formation as a way of changing how the lives and needs of the poor can be better understood.

Evangelistic intent

Our thinking and practice of transforming development must have an evangelistic intent. This needs to be understood with some care. This is not a call for proselytism, nor is it a call to coercive, manipulative or culturally insensitive evangelism. It is not even a call for all development practitioners to become evangelists. No one knows the moment when someone is ready for faith, nor is God limited to the staff of a particular agency in bringing his Good News. Rather, it is a call to be sure we do our development with an attitude of mind that prays and yearns for people to know Jesus Christ.

Development that is Christian must reflect our belief that the best news is neither clean water nor healthy children nor community solidarity, good as all of these are. The best news is that through faith in Christ, anyone can be reconciled with God and be at peace with him and with each other.

In every case study, this commitment is clearly central. Most of the agencies and all of the people in the cases have a clear and unambiguous vision as being development people in Christian mission. The constitution of United Mission to Nepal (chapter 1) declares its mission is "to make Christ known by word and life" and is able to make the claim that "every place where UMN had a project, a church emerged." Mindanao Baptist Rural Life Center (3) declares in its mission statement that it wants "evangelism that results in churches."

The goal of Himalaya Social Service (7) is "to plant the church of Jesus Christ among the poor and needy of the city of Shimla." The criteria for project selection by the Maranatha Trust project in Indonesia require that "projects should be structured in such a way that they reflect and promote an active witness to the

Lordship of Christ and the demands of this Lordship for repentance, faith and a lifestyle of obedience and service" (5).

Social analysis

We need to redevelop our tools of social analysis. When we do needs analysis, we too frequently use the readily available tools of sociology, anthropology, and the like. All of these are flawed because they reflect a world view that limits their scope to the material ("real") world. This has two consequences.

First, we end up with large amounts of information about the material world and little or none about the spiritual realities of people's lives. Our information is about family size, incidence of disease, agricultural productivity, and water contamination. This material analysis tends to lead to material solutions: family planning, immunization, introduction of improved seeds and bore holes.

However, our lack of knowledge about values, religious practices, spiritual oppression and the like limits our development response as Christians. If we truly understand the world as a seamless spiritual-material reality, then the scope of our development research must include both the fear of the demons and the quality of drinking water, the impact both of witchcraft and of poor soil. The Oudong Rural Health case study, for example, does mention the fear of local and ancestral spirits as part of its description of the context of its development work.

Second, because moderns locate cause in the material world and traditional cultures locate it in the unseen or spiritual world, the development process is skewed and only one side's views influence the choice of development activities. This explains why local people don't use the latrines they themselves have built. They were talked into building the latrines on the basis of the germ theory of illness (in the eyes of the development practitioner), while they themselves cannot understand how latrines can help with the real cause of disease—evil spirits.

There was little evidence in our case studies of this dimension of holism. Social analysis, when it was alluded to, appeared to be a separate enterprise from the task of understanding people's spiritual needs. While the Oudong Rural Health project did take note of the role of fear of spirits in the lives of the Khmer, it did not relate this fear to issues of heath nor to World Vision's "scientific" response to health needs.

Holistic evaluations

We need to develop holistic evaluations. We need to go beyond assessing solely the technical side of our work. We need to add some new dimensions to our holistic ministry evaluations.

First, we need to assess whether or not our transforming development has an evangelistic intent. What kind of indicators would help us make this judgement? What is happening in the local churches? Are people more open to the gospel and Christianity? How are the people more aware of the activity of God? How has their view of God changed? How has ours? Are development practitioners prepared and willing to answer questions to which the gospel is the answer? In every one of our case studies, there is information about people who have become Christians. The cases make it clear that the development practitioners are giving gospel answers to the people's questions and the people are listening. It would be interesting to know what has changed regarding the people's understanding of who God is and what the Christian church is for.

Second, we also need to begin asking a new question in our evaluation process: What message are people receiving? When a community health worker participates in an immunization campaign, we must not limit our inquiry to the extent of the immunization coverage. We must also ask how the local people understand immunizations and the cause of their effectiveness. If the answer is either powerful magic or modern medicine, then, they have received effective protection against disease accompanied by an implicit message that is not Christian. This alerts us to the need to work harder on the message that accompanies our development intervention. This is how we can learn our way to better holism. In each of our case studies, it would have been interesting to know how the local people understood or made sense of the development changes going on around them.

Finally, we need to ask, What kind of Christians are we making? This is important in two ways. First, if no one is interested in becoming a Christian, we ought to have the courage to take note of the fact and ask why this might be. While it may be true that it is not yet God's time for these people, it may also be true that no one is encouraging these people to become Christians or that the Christian message they are receiving is either unattractive or not understood. Second, we need to know if people coming to faith in Christ are now reaching out to the poor and lost among them.

In each of our case studies, people are coming to faith in Christ and for this we are thankful to God. It would be interesting to know if these new Christians are men and women who love God and love their neighbors with equal passion or whether we are contributing to the problem of a spiritualized Christianity unconcerned for life in this world—the very problem we are trying to solve in our struggle toward holism.

Reframed interventions

We need to reframe our technical interventions. Holistic evaluations will consistently reveal that our technical work of health care, agriculture, sanitation, water and micro-enterprise development is being understood in ways that are either modern or traditional, but not Christian. This means we need to discover a new set of narratives to accompany our development technology so that it is understood as Christians would wish—as pointing to the activity and character of a loving God who is both concerned for people's welfare and desires to be in personal relationship with them.

The United Mission of Nepal case alludes to this idea when it asks the question, "Was there a way to conceptualize or articulate a vision of hydropower development as part of God's mission, God's redeeming power transforming human society?" Once we begin to understand the words that need to accompany our development technology, every technical professional will need help in becoming aware of his or her functional atheism and then receive training in how to rejoin word and deed so that credit is given to whom credit is due.

Conclusion

At the end of the day we come back to the question, What is holistic ministry? Christian relief and development agencies have tended to select among several different options in their search for holistic ministry.

Some agencies decide that, since they are Christian, the purpose of their development activities should be to create opportunities to carry out their real mission: proclamation of the Good News. This framework makes development a tool for another agenda. Most of our case studies have not operated from this frame, although all desire the Good News to be proclaimed and heard.

Others decide that they are solely in the development business, while the local church or some other part of their organization is to be the source of evangelism. While this may be a practical, and even appropriate, division of labor, it allows the development agency to beg the question. None of our case studies reflect this approach.

Still others, trying to avoid the first two options, opt for the position that carrying out development with Christian staff creates the holism necessary to make development Christian. Staff pray, go to church, tell everyone they are Christian and talk about Jesus. The problem is that their development activities—immunizations, well-digging, and revolving loan funds—are done in ways that are indistinguishable from those done by any secular agency. Most of our cases approach holistic ministry in this way.

My observation is that, while development and evangelism are combined in the activities of the projects and in the lives of the practitioners, there is little evidence of the deeper level of holism I am attempting to articulate in this chapter. There is still a long way to go to conceptualize and find expression for a thoroughly seamless spiritual-physical understanding of holistic ministry.

I do not say this with a critical spirit nor from a position of believing that I or World Vision has a better way, much less a better practice. Rather, I am trying to articulate a problem we all face. We are all carriers of modernity. We have been shaped by it during our schooling and upbringing and in our churches and development training. We are all blind to some extent.

The recovery task is daunting. To call for the reframing of the many disciplines from which development practitioners draw their skills is daunting. To insist on retraining and retooling all of us who have been practitioners over the years is asking a lot. Yet there is no choice. We can either continue to live in cultural captivity to a Western view of modernity and hence act as its missionaries, or return to our roots and ask God's help in recovering his vision for healing and wholeness. Development will never be truly Christian any other way.

NOTES

1   L. Newbigin. *The Gospel in a Pluralist Society*. Grand Rapids: Eerdmans (1989) and L. Sanneh.

2   P. Hiebert. "The Flaw of the Excluded Middle." *Missiology*, X, No. 1 (January 1982)

3   B. Bradshaw. *Bridging the Gap: Development, Evangelism and Shalom*. Monrovia: MARC (1994)

4   M. Scott. "Biblical Reflection and the Work of Development in World Vision Urban Projects." Unpublished evaluation report (Summer 1994).

5   P. Hiebert. "Critical Contextualization." *International Bulletin of Missionary Research*, 11, No. 3 (July 1987).

6   E. Cohen. "The Missionary as Stranger: A Phenomenological Analysis of Christian Missionaries' Encounter with the Folk Religions of Thailand." *Review of Religious Research*, 31, No. 4 (June 1990).

Acknowledgments

This paper is a synthesis of material adapted from a wide range of books and articles combined with many conversations with colleagues around the world. The author is indebted to conversations with Paul Hiebert, Vinay Samuel, Bruce Bradshaw, Kwame Bediako, Saphir Athyal, Jayakumar Christian, John Steward, Ron Sider, Loc Le Chau, Mac Bradshaw, Tom McAlpine, Manfred Grellert and many others.

Part three

Conclusion

13
At the end of the day

Bryant Myers

W hat can we say, at the end of the day, about holistic relief and development ministries? What do these cases teach us? What can we learn from the perspectives of theology, anthropology, modernity, training and NGO management?

It is hard to say; holistic relief and development is a difficult task. The real world reflected in our cases is messy and ambiguous. The cases defy easy analysis and codification. In fact, we damage the life of our experience if we work too hard at sorting it out and summing it up.

I would like to focus on some themes that seem to keep emerging in both the cases and the analytical chapters. My intent in naming these themes is to stimulate further reflection by practitioners as they pursue their calling as Christian relief and development workers. In addition to the cases and the analytical chapters, I will also draw on the record of the meeting in Chiang Mai, the notes Dr. Ted Yamamori calls the "memory" of the consultation.

What follows deliberately tries to avoid the language of models or best approaches, language that so often yields a blueprint for programmatic ministry. As Eddie Elliston so aptly points out in his chapter, personal relationships are the transformative element of Christian ministry. As my friend Jayakumar Christian is fond of pointing out, "Holism is in the person, not the program." That said, I will now discuss seven recurring themes in the case studies:

- Holistic practitioners living incarnationally
- Organizational commitment
- The Bible and life
- Prayer, signs and wonders
- Taking the context seriously
- The role of the church
- Indicators of effective holistic ministry

Holistic practitioners living incarnationally

Repeatedly attention is drawn to the people who are carrying out holistic ministry. Again and again, the cases speak of caring Christians living sacrificially among the people they wish to serve. Transformative relationships are difficult to develop at a distance. Going to the people, learning their language and culture, "living in villages as extension agents propagating the Good News of abundant life,"[1] are echoes throughout our cases.

These people are holistic practitioners.[2] They have a clear vision of their role as being development facilitators doing Christian mission. There is no dichotomy between the two. They believe that development provokes questions to which the gospel is the answer and that an evangelism that deals only with the spiritual dimension of life proclaims a reduced and incomplete gospel. There is no separation between the practitioners' professional and spiritual lives.

Organizational commitment

Holism is also reflected in the mission of the organizations that sent the holistic practitioners to their ministries. The mission of the sending organizations in every case clearly and unambiguously states the intent to do relief and development out of a motivation that people may know the risen Lord and become members of his church. Experience elsewhere suggests that when an organization loses its "evangelistic intent," this eventually works itself out in a growing focus on "development or relief professionalism" and a slowly eroding interest in the spiritual impact of the work.

The Bible and life

The Bible plays a central role in the cases and the analytical chapters. The United Mission of Nepal points to the importance of a Nepali Bible as being instrumental in their church planting. The Issaan Development Foundation speaks of letting the Bible speak for itself and warns of substituting theological statements for the living Word of God. The Mindanao Baptist Rural Life Center uses Bible story telling as a tool for evangelism.[3] The Oudong Rural Health case points to the importance of Bible teaching and exposition by national staff in transforming life and culture. It was Bible study and prayer groups that helped marginalized youth find a new cultural place in Sri Lanka.

Our modern world view imprisons the Bible in the spiritual realm, limiting its use to spiritual development. We must free the Bible to work in the material world as well and see it as a tool for transforming human development. Paul Hiebert's chapter reminds us that we must also allow the Bible to speak for itself by allowing the local people to "formulate their own theological responses to the problems they face based on their study of the Scriptures together."

Prayer, signs and wonders

The cases and the "memory" of the meeting repeatedly refer to the importance of prayer. Ted Yamamori notes this in his chapter. The Oudong Rural Health project (chapter 4) is unintelligible without an account of the role of prayer. The case of Kandy City Mission (6) speaks of the importance of seeing "the power of prayer at work." The account of the meeting in Chiang Mai shows that "wasting more time with God" and increasing our emphasis on God are among the things the participants want to do differently in the future.

Signs and wonders also play a role in two of the cases (4, 7). The supernatural work of God in the midst of people who believe in the reality of the spirit world is a way God testifies to himself and his power. We are reminded of something very important in the Oudong case (4) when Phany declares, "I can pray for her [a possessed woman] in Jesus' name, but I have no magic." In Acts 14:8, Paul healed a man without referring to God or Christ, and the next thing he knew the crowd was preparing sacrifices to him. When signs and wonders happen, we must be more like Peter in Acts 3:12: "Why do you stare at us as if by our own power or godliness we had made this man walk?"

One further word of caution. Attributing a supernatural act to God is not enough. It does little good if people who used to go to shamans for charms and to witches for curses, now go to church because they believe Jesus is a more powerful shaman. Substituting Christian magic for traditional magic is hardly a gospel response. We must be sure that signs and wonders are accompanied by a genuine encounter with Jesus and, through him, with the God of the Bible. The truth of the gospel must always accompany the power of the gospel.

Taking the context seriously

There was a great deal of welcome evidence that practitioners of holistic ministry are working harder at bridging the gap between their world and that of the local village or urban setting. Calls for language learning and the great cost of not knowing the local language came through clearly. Issaan Development Foundation (2) went further, in describing its role to "enable Jesus Christ to be born into the Northeast Thai culture." There were calls for "clothing the gospel" in appropriate forms of worship in Thailand (2) and Nepal (1). Paul Hiebert reminds us that such contextualization must be done critically so that we affirm what is good and advocate the transformation of what is sinful.

The role of the church

Where there were local churches, working through them was considered important (2, 3, 5). Where there was no church, the mission doing Christian relief and development saw a local church as their ultimate goal (1, 7). This recognizes the important principle that the local church is the living body of Christ in the area; parachurch agencies are part of the church but are not the church in themselves.

The account of the Chiang Mai meeting does not reveal any consistent pattern in the relationship between the parachurch agency and the local churches. In some cases, people viewed the local church in a more favorable light as a result of the development work done in the village. In other cases, the parachurch development agency plays a positive role in helping the local church take the material needs of the local people more seriously. Sometimes, it was less risky for the development agency to take on the role of working among the poor.

At the same time, the consultation recognized that the presence of the parachurch agency sometimes creates problems for the local church. The higher salaries and perceived status of parachurch agencies often lure younger church leaders away from the church. Sometimes, the local people are tempted to transfer their loyalty to the parachurch agency or even begin to think less respectfully of local churches that seem unable to do what the parachurch agencies do. Governments sometimes fear the combination of foreign money and work among the poor, and express this fear by persecuting the local churches.

God gives gifts to all parts of the body of Christ, and the purpose of these gifts is to build up the whole body. A great deal more work needs to be done in thinking through and finding new models for the relationship between parachurch groups and local churches. Each needs the other; each must build up the other.

Indicators of effective holistic ministry

The account of the Chiang Mai consultation reveals a lot of work invested in deciding what the indicators of a genuinely holistic ministry might be. A consensus emerged for three types of indicators:

- People have opportunities to respond to the good news of Jesus Christ. If there is no proclamation from some source—the local church, other mission groups or the relief and development agency—then there is no holism. The conference agreed on the need for Christian presence, patience, practice and proclamation.

- There is evidence of lasting value change or transformation. These may include reconciliation, freedom from fear of spirits, love, joy, hope, patience, gentleness, sharing, greater concern for the environment and concern for those on the margin of society. The Maranatha Trust case places great emphasis on their Value Formation Seminar.

- There is transformation of societal structures, institutions and processes. This may include changes in oppressive structures like the caste system or a place for young people who once joined an insurrection. Of the indicators of holistic ministry, this one was the least developed. Clearly, evangelicals still have a way to go in developing their understanding of the gospel's demand that political and economic structures be for life and for people, and, when they are not, that the church is to assume a prophetic role and call these structures into account.

At the end of the day, our understanding of holistic ministry is a little clearer, yet still incomplete. Listening to our experience always clarifies and creates new questions, at the same time. Like everything else a Christian does, holistic ministry needs to be done in faith, trusting that God will take our small offering among the poor and the lost and, in his grace and time, transform it into another small piece of his emerging kingdom on earth.

Amen.

NOTES

1   The quotation is from chapter three, the case study of Mindanao Baptist Rural Life Center, Philippines.

2   I first heard this phrase from Dr. Sam Kamaleson of World Vision International.

3   Chronological Bible Storying is a highly effective tool for use among traditional cultures with strong oral traditions. The idea was developed by Trevor McIlwain and Dell Schultze of New Tribes Mission. *The Bible Storying Newsletter* is available from Southern Baptist missionary J. O. Terry, Media Consultant for Asia and the Pacific, 2 Marine Vista, 20-75 Neptune Court, Singapore 1544.

Part four

Appendixes

Appendix A:
Consultation participants

S ome fifty practitioners, theorists and observers gathered in Chiang Mai, Thailand, in November 1994 to discuss effective holistic ministry in Asia. Following is a list of the participants, their affiliations and the countries in which they are based.

Name	Organization	Country
Simon Batchelor	Christian Outreach	Cambodia
Tri Budiardjo	World Vision	Cambodia
David Bussau	Maranatha Trust	Australia
Tim Byers	Intl Technical Assistance Group	Thailand
Dave Conner	Food for the Hungry	Thailand
Paul De Neui	Lower Issaan Foundation	Thailand
Stephen Dowall	Southeast Asian Outreach	Cambodia
Steve Ferguson	Fieldstead & Company	U.S.A.
David Fitzstevens	World Vision	Thailand
Mike and Jane Fucella	Fellowship Church of Sivilai	Thailand
Kabi Gangmei	NEICORD	India
Scott Geisinger	YWAM	India
Steve Goode	YWAM	Thailand
Fred Gregory	World Concern	U.S.A.
James Gustafson	Issaan Development Foundation	Thailand
Cristina Houtz	Fieldstead & Company	U.S.A.
Gregg Keen	World Concern	Cambodia
Paul Kennel	World Concern	Thailand

Name	Organization	Country
Rob Martin	First Fruit Inc.	U.S.A.
Thomas McCallie III	The Maclellan Foundation	U.S.A.
Marty Melvin	World Christian Magazine	U.S.A.
S.J. and O.E. Mesach	Bethel Church of Indonesia	Indonesia
Ed Metzler	United Mission to Nepal	Nepal
Jeff Palmer	Mindanao Baptist Rural Life Ctr	Philippines
Jacob Perera	FRIDSRO	Sri Lanka
Truc Pham	CAMA Services	Thailand
Priyadi Reksasiswaya	Duta Bina Bhuana Foundation	Indonesia
Walter Ridgley	Food for the Hungry	Laos
David/Yupin Riggins	Food for the Hungry	Thailand
Kathereeya Robertson	Food for the Hungry	Thailand
Elgin Saha	HEED	Bangladesh
Vinay Samuel	Oxford Ctr for Mission Studies	U.K.
Eriana Sany	Universitas Kristen Immanuel	Indonesia
Debbie Sayo	Food for the Hungry	Philippines
Don/Diana Schmierer	Fieldstead & Company	U.S.A.
Waluyo Sejati	GKJ Salib Purtih	Indonesia
Philip Scott	YWAM	Thailand
Margot Sluka	World Vision	Cambodia
George Stephen	Presbyterian Church	Sri Lanka
Don Stephens	Mercy Ships, YWAM	U.S.A.
David Tegenfeldt	World Concern	Thailand
Rick/Carla Thompson	World Christian Magazine	U.S.A.
Bryan Truman	World Vision	Thailand
Ted Yamamori	Food for the Hungry	U.S.A.

Appendix B:
Case study guidelines

Holistic ministry practitioners attending the November 1994 consultation in Chiang Mai, Thailand, wrote case studies of effective holistic ministry in Asia. The authors used the following five guidelines:

1. Acquaint yourself with the concept of holistic ministry

Although reconciliation with man is not reconciliation with God, nor is social action evangelism, nor is political liberation salvation, nevertheless we affirm that evangelism and sociopolitical involvement are both part of our Christian duty.

Both are necessary expressions of our doctrines of God and man, our love for our neighbor and our obedience to Jesus Christ (see section five of the Lausanne Covenant). Tetsunao Yamamori expresses this concept as follows:

> Ministering to physical needs and ministering to spiritual needs, though functionally *separate*, are relationally *inseparable*, and both are *essential* to the total ministry of Christ's church.

2. Provide the context of your case study by giving its historical background

How did the development project get started? What type of a development project (water, food production, health, micro-enterprise, integrated development)? When and how did it begin? Among whom?

3. Describe the process of people coming to know Christ

What happened here? As a result of lifestyle evangelism of some individual staff members? As a result of a specific evangelistic strategy of your organization? As a result of your partnership with a local church?

Were there dynamic individuals who played a key role in bringing people to Christ? Give details. How many people accepted Christ? Who actually came to accept Christ? As individuals, families, or as villagers together?

4. Identify factors which contributed to the emergence of a Christ group (a church or a group of believers)

Why did people come to know Christ through the development project in which you were engaged? Were there any specific decisions made by individuals or your organization which resulted in the conversion of people? What was your own part in the result of the case?

5. Make your own evaluation of the case

Looking at the case, are there things you would or should have done to improve the result? What do you think were some obstacles which retarded the progress of the spiritual ministry?